IN THE
FLOW OF LIFE

Also by Eric Butterworth

Discover the Power Within You

Spiritual Economics

Unity: A Quest for Truth

Celebrate Yourself!

The Concentric Perspective

*MetaMorality: A Metaphysical Approach to
the Ten Commandments*

*The Universe Is Calling: Opening to the
Divine Through Prayer*

Life Is for Living

Life Is for Loving

IN THE
FLOW OF LIFE

ERIC
BUTTERWORTH

UNITY® Books

Unity Village, MO 64065

To receive a catalog of all our Unity publications (books, cassettes, compact discs, and magazines) or to place an order, call our Customer Service Department: (816) 969-2069 or 1-800-669-0282.

Cover photograph © Carr CLIFTON
Cover photograph of Salmon River, Idaho
Cover design by Chad Pio

Library of Congress Catalog Card Number: 82-50121
ISBN 0-87159-066-2
Canada BN 13252 9033 RT

Unity Books feels a sacred trust to be a healing presence in the world. By printing with biodegradable soybean ink on recycled paper, we believe we are doing our part to be wise stewards of our Earth's resources.

Contents

Preface
to the
1994 Edition

About twenty years ago a word came into vogue in scientific treatises, psychological journals, and conversations of people in the street. The word was *flow*. It was used in many contexts, from the more esoteric idea of a Universe in "flux," to the personal comment on the human condition "I am really in the flow!" And it reached a high point in whimsy in a cartoon in *The New Yorker*, depicting two grand ladies standing beneath a life-sized portrait of an obvious "gentleman of distinction." The caption read: "And I said to my husband, 'Go with the flow!' and he went."

But this insight into the "flow of life" is no laughing matter. It is an explanation and articulation of a very basic process of life in the Universe.

I have no way of knowing if the theme of this widely read book (first published in 1975) contributed to this "rage" or whether my thinking was influenced by it. I do know that this concept of the flow of life and expressions such as "go with the flow" have been a constant theme in my teaching for more than half a century. But however the idea came about, it is an important discovery in the quest for understanding by anyone in search of the Truth.

I am delighted to add this preface to the new edition of *In the Flow of Life* if only to rearticulate my great enthusiasm for the study of the basic "flow of the Universe." Listen well to the theme of Plotinus that if you flow as life flows, you need no other power. Anything is evil that blocks the flow of creative action, and everything is healthy that flows with the Universe. It will serve you well to work with this theme in your practice of Truth. It could be the most important influence in your life.

With an objectivity that the passage of time allows, I have been re-experiencing the book myself, this time as a student—which I most certainly am. I am finding the message to be helpful and extremely relevant to life in the world today. A serious effort to apply the principles of "the flow of life" is doing great things for me. And I sincerely feel that it will work wonders for you too.

In our classroom work with this theme, we have used a mantralike chant in meditation: "I'm in the flow of life, I am, I am, I am, I am; I'm in the flow of life." After repeating this for a few times, we make it more personally significant by singing "I am the flow of life, I am the flow of life, I am, I am, I am, I am; I am the flow of life."

Have many good days in your adventure in Truth ... and "go with the flow."

Eric Butterworth
New York City, New York
June 1993

Introduction

To induce the reader to continue beyond the first page, it is normally assumed that a book should give promise of helpful information to come. Why would a book be written and published if not to inform? There may be many reasons. For instance, this book was not written to inform but to "outform." By this, I mean that I am not concerned with putting ideas into your mind but with awakening your superconscious awareness in which all things are known.

Information is knowledge received by tuition. "Outformation" is wisdom unfolded by intuition and flowing forth into manifestation in your body and affairs. I hope to excite your mind with some helpful insights. An insight, however, is like the food you eat. To become energy, food is transformed by the process of metabolism. We do not become the food we eat; it turns into us.

My goal is not to transfer the "gems of wisdom" from these printed pages into your mind. The insights shared, which I believe will be helpful, must be transmuted into a consciousness of the flow of the creative process. One could memorize every word of the book and be able to repeat it by rote, paragraph by paragraph, and in the end he would have an overloaded mind, and possibly even, as Unity co-founder Charles Fillmore suggests, an uncomfortable experience of "metaphysical indigestion."

It is a common motivation to look for information by which to set things right. However, people are not in the world to set it right but to see it rightly. Jesus said, "The kingdom of heaven is at hand" (Mt. 3:2 Revised Standard Version, as are all Bible quotations in this book unless otherwise noted), but it is right seeing that is the key to experiencing it. In fact, right seeing leads to an actual *outforming* of it.

A word of advice: Don't read this book as if it were a novel, even if its novel approach entices you to read on. The information contained herein can be gathered easily at one reading. But the outformation in your life that it is intended to elicit may take a lifetime. Pause frequently to reflect and meditate, to digest spiritually.

I am not dealing with religion in a theological sense, but with the transcendence of life. Thus I have no desire to proselytize or to convert you. Paul says, "Don't let the world around you squeeze you into its own mold, but let God remold your minds from within" (Rom. 12:2 Phillips). If you can just get into the flow of the universe within you, you will experience an immediacy of the Presence of God and a clarity of mind. This is likely what Jesus had in mind when He said, "Blessed are the pure in heart, for they shall see God" (Mt. 5:8).

The word *eye* comes from a Sanskrit root word which means "fountain." This is beautifully significant, for when your mind is remolded from within, you are synchronized with the omnipresent flow of God which streams out in the very act of seeing. You see *from* the consciousness of God. Thus you actually project this consciousness toward anything your *eye* beholds.

> That thou seest, man, become too thou
>   must;
> God, if thou seest God, dust if thou seest
>   dust.
> —Father Angelus

What you see you become, because of the outforming process of mind. So, perhaps you can understand why I am not interested in simply informing you about Truth but in awakening in you a consciousness of the dynamic flow of life, that you may experience a progressive outforming of this flow in creative and dynamic ways in every phase of your life.

CHAPTER 1

Living Life
From
Within-Out

You are about to embark upon an adventure into the inner world of mind and Spirit. It could be the most important journey in consciousness you have ever taken. It should be inspiring. It is intended to be challenging. You may also find it disturbing.

If you have a fixed belief about the reality of life, a "custom-made" set of convictions, then you may want to turn back, for your every settled view will be challenged. Your whole world will be turned upside down and inside out. But in the end, if you keep on until you catch on, you will gain a new perspective of life that will lead to a new experience in living.

It has been said that the starting point in spiritual realization is a right understanding of that One designated as the Almighty. But in a world of such broad diversity, how can we understand unity? How can we discover the One without lapsing into a duality that implies *two*?

There are many definitions of God, but none

quite so insightful as this: *God is a sphere whose center is everywhere and whose circumference is nowhere.* It is not a picture that can be drawn. In fact, it should draw the mind away from the tendency to envision an anthropomorphic being.

A sphere whose center is everywhere? Impossible! But wait: if the center is everywhere, it must be where I am. Could this be the meaning of omnipresence? A point of life and light, present everywhere *as* each individualized expression? If this is true, then I am the center of God. It is an audacious thought with a sacrilegious tone. And yet, can a geographical center be otherwise located in a dynamic and expanding universe? Every point in this sphere, which is God, is thus a bubbling forth of the infinite flow of life.

What is the One that we call God? It is not a One off there somewhere, ruling the universe as an absentee landlord. It is *the One*, the whole of things, the allness of which and in which I am an *eachness*. No matter what I may think I am, I am the flowing forth of *the One*.

I am unique and different at the surface. There can be no other "eachness" quite like me. And yet I have no existence outside of the whole. My eachness can never be separated from the allness which is God. The Greeks said, "Man, know thyself." I can only know the One as I know myself as the self-livingness of the One. But I can only really know myself when I know that I am "in the flow of life."

Let's examine the prevailing attitudes about this thing called life. There are two basic views: (1) We come into the world as empty creatures who go forth in life to be filled. Life for us at any time is the sum of what has happened to us and what we have been able to accumulate in wisdom, experience, or things. (2) We come into the world as living souls of infinite potentiality to be discovered and released, for life is lived from within-out.

The first view has been predominant through the ages. Every person has felt its conditioning to some extent, for it is the "wisdom of the world." Subtly but certainly, we are trained to think of life as a "getting" experience. Like Buddhist monks, we are given the psychological counterpart of the little begging bowl by which to go out into the world to seek the "gifts of God" from our parents, our schools, our religion, and our work. No matter what we hunger or desire, we invariably go begging "out there" for fulfillment. Paul seemed to know better. In 2 Timothy 1:6, he writes, "I remind you to rekindle the gift of God that is within you."

Søren Kierkegaard, founder of existentialism, was strongly influenced by his own vision of the inner "flow." He talks of an Arab in the desert suddenly discovering a spring in his tent, providing a constant flow of water in abundance. And he says that we have the same feeling of security and well-being when, after years of living a life from the outside, thinking that happiness comes from out

11

there, we finally turn inward and discover the source within. It is probably true that most people attempt to live their life from the outside-in. Life for them is almost totally determined by what happens around them or to them. Ask them, "How are you?" and they are reluctant to answer until they consult the news of the day, check on the Dow-Jones averages, get the weather report, or appraise the mood of their family or their office associates. Their life is almost totally "outer-directed." And they are caught up in the dilemma of whether to conform to the world outside or to spend their life resisting it.

The great Truth taught by the mystics of all ages is: *Life is lived from within-out*. This means that the whole universe is concentrated at the point where you are. More than this—you are the universe expressing as you. You are its living enterprise. It forever stands behind you with its full resources. However, the fullness of this universal support comes *through* you and not just *to* you. The most profound knowledge that you can attain is that your whole existence flows forth inexorably from a universal process, which is always from within-out. How widespread and deep-seated is the belief that we are forever in competition with people and in conflict with the world around us. Our fears, resentment, anger, even grief come because we feel that the instability of life in the world is a threat to our existence in it. Jesus gave the answer, "The kingdom of God is within you" (Lk. 17:21 KJV). This is an absolutely amazing concept. Unfortunately, few have grasped its implications, looking upon it as a deferred payment into the begging bowl.

What is this mystical kingdom? It is the focus of the universe upon, and the flow of the universe within, humankind. This is made unmistakably clear as Jesus said, "It is your Father's good pleasure to give you the kingdom" (Lk. 12:32). In other words, there is a longing at the heart of the universe to flow forth into and to perfect all that has been created. This is the basis of all healing and success and overcoming. The kingdom within is the realm of all-potentiality, all-substance, all-life, all-love, all-peace. Jesus said: "Do not be anxious about your life .... But seek first his kingdom and... all these things shall be yours as well" (Mt. 6:25, 33). In other words, get into the flow and you will receive all that you desire or need.

This is not at all a new concept. It wasn't new with Jesus. In the fifth century B.C., Heraclitus, a Greek philosopher, was teaching that "all is flux, nothing stays still."[1] And a full century earlier in ancient China, Lao-Tzu was teaching that the human spirit has its source in the divine fountain which must be permitted to flow freely through man. He believed that anyone who flows "as life flows" has solved the enigma of human existence and needs no other power. He felt that anything is evil that blocks the flow of creative action, and everything is healthy that flows with the universe.

It is this concept of the "flow" that sets Emerson apart as America's most influential essayist. Academicians never know what to do with him. He doesn't quite fit the labels of "religionist" or "philosopher," so he is called a transcendentalist. But by whatever term he is called, he is not to be ignored. Here is one good reason:

> There is a principle which is the basis of things, which all speech aims to say, and all action to evolve, a simple, quiet, undescribed, undescribable presence, dwelling very peacefully in us, our rightful lord: we are not to do, but to let do; not to work, but to be worked upon; and to this homage there is a consent of all thoughtful and just men in all ages and conditions. To this sentiment belong vast and sudden enlargements of power. . . . We are one day to deal with real being,—essences with essences.[2]

Emerson could not understand why we make life such a problem by frustrating the flow of good. He said: "Our life might be much easier and simpler than we make it; the world might be a happier place than it is; there is no need of struggles, convulsions, and despairs, of the wringing of hands and gnashing of teeth. We miscreate our own evils. We interfere with nature."

In my book *Unity of All Life*, I tell the story of a man who sat brooding at his desk one evening after receiving his dismissal notice from a company he had served for more than twenty years.[3] He was reflecting in despair on the difficulty of getting another job at his age, the impossible task of living on his income, and the shock of feeling that he was no longer needed, that he was useless, through, washed-up.

He noticed a spider on the desk and unconsciously brushed it off. Suddenly he was watching in awe as the tiny creature automatically spun a strand to bear its weight and swung gracefully to the floor. He began to wonder: If this tiny creature could get into the flow of a mysterious resource and deal so creatively with its crisis, then why could he not do the same? The answer came dramatically: He must have gotten out of his own natural flow or this situation could not have come to him. The fact that he was so disturbed by it proved this to be true. Now, getting himself synchronized in consciousness with the flow in the realization that his good did not come *to* him but *through* him might not get his job back, but it would most certainly move him inexorably forward to something better.

With a new consciousness of the flow and with mind and body processes synchronized with the flow, the man went on to new security and creativity. He had always longed for the opportunity to write. Now was his chance, and write he did! Not that he became a Hemingway, but he wrote and sold much that he wrote. And along with his retirement income, he managed to achieve an economic security that he had never known. All this because he was now consciously and joyously in the flow.

This idea of the flow of life from within is not easy to grasp, for most of our wisdom and experience, gleaned from the world about us, would seem to contradict it. Emerson says that we must unlearn the wisdom of the world, lie low in the divine circuits, and by so doing, open the door by which the affluence of heaven and Earth streams into us. He is not suggesting that we forsake the cumulative wisdom of science. He refers to those facts that lead to limitation.

David Sarnoff, back in the early 1950s, called his researchers into his office and ordered them to produce a videotape process in black and white and compatible color. The men were speechless with the sheer audacity of such an impossible assignment. As they left the room, one of them was heard to mutter under his breath, "It must be wonderful to have an imagination so completely unrestrained by a knowledge of the facts." However, they did unlearn their great wisdom, and the television you watch today has evolved from their creative achievement.

We have been misled into believing that the accumulation of the world's wisdom makes us wise, whereas actually it may only make us prejudiced. This is why Jesus said, "You will know the truth, and the truth will make you free" (Jn. 8:32). Free from the thought of living at the mercy of the world outside, free to "let God be God" in us, and free to get into the flow of the universe of life, light, and substance.

It is significant to note that Jesus did *not* say, "You will know *about* Truth." Knowledge about Truth may simply be more wisdom of the world to be unlearned. He specifically said, "You will know the truth." At the risk of appearing boastful, may I say that I know a lot about Truth, and I have a vast library of books and many file drawers of notes to prove it. However, if I am confronted with a personal challenge, all this is as so much excess baggage. Face to face with life and alone with myself, I am left with only what I *know*. This is not a repertoire of words or statements that I can quickly call to mind but the simple faith to *be still and know that I am in the flow.*

One point to get clear in mind in the very beginning of any study of Truth is this: Truth is not just words or affirmations or books or teachings. Truth is a universal flow that can only be vaguely caught in the web of human consciousness. Theology, whether traditional or metaphysical, tends to crystallize Truth and thus obstruct the flow. It is as if we consider an empty fist as containing something real and a pointing finger as the object pointed at. If we point to the moon and then revere the finger as if it were the moon, we have lost the idea. "Truth words," even the great utterances of master teachers, simply point to the reality of the universe that can only be experienced firsthand as a flow from within ourselves.

> Truth is within ourselves; it takes no rise
> From outward things, whate'er you may
>   believe.
> There is an inmost centre in us all,
> Where truth abides in fulness; and around,
> Wall upon wall, the gross flesh hems it in,
> This perfect, clear perception—which is
>   truth.
> A baffling and perverting carnal mesh
> Binds it, and makes all error: and, to
>   KNOW,
> Rather consists in opening out a way
> Whence the imprisoned splendor may
>   escape,
> Than in effecting entry for a light
> Supposed to be without.[4]
> —Robert Browning

The student of the "new insight in Truth" often quotes Emmet Fox by saying, "Life is consciousness." It is a great concept that has helped many persons to change their way of thinking and living. However, there is so much more involved than is normally recognized. "Consciousness" is not just what we may be thinking about consciously. It is also the deeper-than-conscious thought accumulation in the subconscious mind. And it refers to the relationship we have with the allness of God-Mind and the degree to which we have laid claim to it.

"Consciousness" is not just what we have put into our minds. It is also the degree to which we have discovered and released our own "imprisoned splendor" and gotten into the flow. This subtle distinction becomes dramatic when we realize that, no matter what level of consciousness we may be on at a given moment, there is always more within; the allness of God is within. We may be in the consciousness of illness or lack or inharmony or injustice, and yet right where we are, we can be still and acknowledge oneness with the creative process and "out of his heart shall flow rivers of living water" (Jn. 7:38). We are never farther from this healing flow than the "consent" to let it unfold.

If we follow the "half-truth" that we are what we have put into our minds, we will be deluded into dealing with education on the basis of the "begging bowl"—feeding learning into the mind. In olden times we said, jokingly but in earnest, "Slam it in, cram it in, children's heads are hollow." Education, dealt with out of the consciousness of the flow, is a perversion of the creative process.

Socrates referred to education as withdrawing wisdom from within the mind of the child out to where he or she could examine and use that which was his or her own from the beginning. And Carlyle refers to genius as an uttering forth of the inspired soul of a human being. He insists that this inspired soul exists potentially in every person, that it is comparatively independent of education or training, and that it awaits the inspiration that we call genius.

It is tragic in our day that we fail to introduce the child to the idea and process of the Superconscious Mind, and to lead that child to experience the flow of the universal force within. The new era that is very much upon us calls for people who have been adequately prepared by "soul training." Permitting the flow of universal power to direct the conscious mind is imperative if we want to rise to the full potential of our genius.

The same "half-truth" that we are what we have put into the mind leads many persons to use the popular technique of "programming the mind" with mental patterns of health and success. Now, it is true that "Thou dost keep him in perfect peace, whose mind is stayed on thee" (Is. 26:3). But this certainly does not say that we can have peace only by putting thoughts of peace into the mind. Mind programming tends to assume that we can only be healthy if we feed thoughts of health into the mind. This is a denial of the natural healing force of life.

It could lead toward the unwarranted assumption of the responsibility for the wellness of the body. "Working" constantly and anxiously for the heart, the stomach, the eyes, and so forth, one may become a veritable "metaphysical hypochondriac." How much better to know with Lao-tzu that *every-thing is healthy that flows with the universe.* In the face of any kind of disorder, the need is to get into the flow, to release the "imprisoned splendor" of Truth from within, instead of trying to "effect entry for a light supposed to be without."

Much stress is given to the "art of demonstration." This is good, for through knowledge of the working of spiritual law, we can rise to a new level of health and success. However, if we do not build on the consciousness of our source in the universal flow of life, we try to make the law work for us in the form of the good we desire. Actually, there is no way we can make divine law work for us or for anyone. Can we influence gravity to work for us or the sun to shine for us? All we can or need to do is get into a right relationship with them.

What is called the "law of healing" is simply the eternal flow of life that is present as an allness even within an illness. The "law of success" is simply the flow of ideas and creativity that can turn failure into productivity and lack into abundance. We do not make the law work through prayer or treatment. Divine law is always working, even if we may be frustrating its flow through our attitudes and actions.

Through what Teilhard calls "the unimpeachable wholeness of the universe," wherever you are
and whatever may be the need, God is with you;
the whole universe stands behind you to a degree
equal to the full extent of the need. All the powers
of heaven and Earth are with you, working on your
side, on the side of healing, of justice, of overcoming. Ella Wheeler Wilcox catches this great idea in
her lines:

> That which the upreaching spirit can
>   achieve
> The grand and all creative forces know;
> They will assist and strengthen as the light
> Lifts up the acorn to the oak-tree's height.
> Thou has but to resolve, and lo! God's
>   whole
> Great universe shall fortify thy soul.[5]

You do not need to *make* a demonstration, and
in fact you cannot. There is no use trying to make
divine law work for you, for the law is an inexorable
flow. You are always in this flow—as you are
always in gravity and it is always in you. You may,
and often do, get out of the awareness of the flow.
But the need is to cease doing whatever is interfer-
ing with the natural flow of your good from within.
Turn your thoughts from tension and strain. Let go
and let the flow of life unfold.

From one of the aphorisms of Patanjali, we find this great Truth revealed:

As the removal of earth by a farmer
digging a ditch
Opens up a channel for water to flow
to his crops,
So the removal of obstacles by the student
opens up
A channel for Cosmic Energy to flow
into his being.

This is not to negate the idea of positive thinking. We are thinking creatures, and it is as true now as when Solomon said it: "For as he thinketh in his heart, so is he" (Prov. 23:7 KJV).

However, we need a clearer understanding of the role of thought in consciousness. Thought of itself does not create. It either places us consciously in the universal flow or it frustrates the flow. If we think sickness or lack, we do not manufacture these things. When the thought is out of synchronization with the flow of life, then, even as anything cut off from its source, we "come to know want."

In the same sense, if we think health or abundance, we do not create these things. There is no way that man can create health. It is a flow or "flowering" of divine life. When the mind is stayed on the God-thought of wholeness, we are synchronized with the flow of life. When we think abundance, we are synchronized with the flow of abundance. We do not create it nor do we start or stop the flow. We simply accept it, giving our "consent" to its natural flow. This is what the presence of God really is—the life of God present in us as an inexorable flow.

And this is what prayer really is—the kind of thought that is synchronized with the flow. Prayer is normally thought of as something you say or do to God or the process of putting affirmations or statements of Truth into the mind. There is so much more. Prayer is a kind of lifting the eyes above the limitations that result from the frustration of the flow to an awareness of the everpresence of the transcendent flow.

When the weather vane points to the north, it does not make the north wind blow. It simply records that the north wind is blowing. In the same sense, when we speak words of Truth in prayer, we do not move God or awaken divine law. Prayer is not putting things into the mind but releasing power from within the mind. It is the highest experience of living life from within-out.

Jesus urged that, in prayer, we go into the "inner chamber" and shut the door. Here there is no one to impress with elaborate prayers; for, as He says, God knows what we have in mind even before we put it into words. Thus there is no need for "vain repetition" or affirmations or prayer statements. An affirmation of Truth is not intended to make something true. It is an effective means of synchronizing our consciousness with the flow of life. Knowing this, there is no intensity or human will involved. We voice the statement of Truth like a feather on the breeze. For it is simply our consent, our way of saying yes to the flow, which is "the Father's good pleasure" in us and for us.

Jesus said, "In the world you have tribulation; but . . . I have overcome the world" (Jn. 16:33). In the world of human experience, we so easily get out of the consciousness of the flow of Spirit. Someone cuts in front of our car on the freeway. How natural it is to be angry! An empty cab sails by, ignoring our frantic waving from the curb, and of course, we are furious. It is perfectly understandable, for this is what life "out there" is about. Or, so we say. But there is no automatic response to conditions. Fear and worry and anger are conditioned reflexes to outside stimuli. When we really know that life is lived from within-out, then no matter what happens around us or to us, we can always get into the transcendent flow from within us. And this is to "overcome the world."

Jesus said, "Love your enemies and pray for those who persecute you, so that you may be sons of your Father" (Mt. 5:44-45). But how can we do that after what they have done? They certainly don't deserve love. That may well be true, but it is irrelevant. The point is, by indulging in enmity, no

matter what the provocation, we lose our consciousness of the flow. The need, then, is to
become re-established in the consciousness of this
inward-out flow of life. This is what Jesus meant
when He said "that you may be sons of your
Father." Why destroy ourselves because of what
someone else has done or not done? This is
precisely what we do when we frustrate the creative power of love. Jesus was saying, "Let go—
and let flow!"

Could it be that the word *flow* has given rise to
the word *flower*, a beautiful symbol of the
unobstructed flow of life? Someone has said, "You
can trust a universe that creates flowers." Now you
can see why Jesus would say, "Consider the lilies,
how they grow; they neither toil nor spin; yet I tell
you, even Solomon in all his glory was not arrayed
like one of these" (Lk. 12:27). Take time occasionally to meditate on a flower, identifying with the
unobstructed flow that is expressing in such fra-
grance and beauty and symmetry. This is the way
life should express for you—the way it most certainly will express when you are consciously in the
flow.

So this is the starting point of our adventure.
Dwell much on this concept that life is lived from
inside-out, and that you are a dynamic center in the
creative flow which is God, and that you have a
built-in capacity for health and success. You can be
more, you can do more, and you can have more in

life because you are inexorably linked to the transcendent flow of life.

Among the ancients, none gives evidence of a clearer concept of the flow than Plotinus. He suggests a mental discipline that might well become the closing assignment for this first chapter. In a few moments of meditation consider this paraphrasing of his words:

Let your mind and heart release all that disturbs you. Let your body be still, and all the frettings of your body, and all that surrounds it; let the earth and sea and air be still and heaven itself; and then think of Spirit as streaming, pouring, rushing, and shining into you, through you, and out from you in all directions while you sit quiet.

CHAPTER 2

The

Healing Stream

"Some people get all the breaks!" How often this cry is heard from the self-pitying or the sympathetic! And it would appear to be true. It has been proved that certain people are "accident prone," while others are always stumbling onto everything from exciting jobs to interesting vacation spots. The Egyptians have a saying about the person who always "falls in the river and comes up with a fish in his mouth."

Certainly it would appear that some people are always getting into or out of sickness, while others are always in good health. Some people are victims of the seasonal contagions that "make the rounds," while others are untouched, referring to themselves as "disgustingly healthy."

It is as if some people are on the right and others on the wrong side of life. But are there right and wrong sides of life? Are some people doomed to lives of pain and suffering because they happen not to be born on the right side? Richard Rumbold, commenting on the political aspect of the question, once cried out: "I never could believe that Providence had sent a few men into the world, ready booted and spurred to ride, and millions ready saddled and bridled to be ridden."[1]

All down through the ages and until comparatively recent times, when sickness appeared in the flesh, the cause was thought to be, almost without exception, in the flesh itself. It was just bad luck or God's will or "the way things are." So the person made no attempt to be other than what he or she believed himself or herself to be; and sadly, sickness was part of what was believed to be. It has been 3000 years since Solomon said, "For as he thinketh in his heart, so is he" (Prov. 23:7 KJV), but it has been a long time getting through to man that "bad luck" is simply a "bad mental habit."

Medicine has been slow to accept the influence of attitudes and emotions on the function of the body. However, the weight of much valid research in the field of psychosomatic causes of illness has become increasingly undeniable. Today doctors are coming to accept as a fact of life the evidence that many ills are emotionally induced or, at least, influenced. There are those who say that 50 percent of all illness is EII (emotionally induced illness). Others say it is more like 90 percent. However, more and more doctors are accepting the revolutionary idea that "all disease is psychosomatic in origin" and that the secret of healing of any kind is to correct the conditions that are impeding the natural flow of life by altering states of consciousness.

In John 21:1-6, there is an episode in which Jesus teaches through a "living parable." The disciples, who were mostly fishermen, were plying their trade on the Sea of Galilee. After a whole night of work, they had caught nothing. At daylight they returned to shore, tired and discouraged. They came upon Jesus who suggested they try again, but that this time they should "cast the net on the right side of the boat." Just imagine their reaction! After all, they were experienced fishermen. What could the carpenter know? And yet, after all they had seen, how could they question His insights? So, they cast out their net as He suggested, and now they were not able to haul it in for all the fish.

The story dramatically symbolizes the right and wrong sides of life. As Shakespeare said, "The fault . . . is not in our stars, but in ourselves, that we are underlings."[2] It is a matter of consciousness and not in the will of God or the fickle finger of fate, and consciousness can be changed. The disciples, in consciousness, were out of the flow of life. By the sheer act of casting from the other side of the boat, they changed their whole experience. This means that by the device of turning in thought from negative to positive, from moods of insufficiency to attitudes of confidence, one may alter one's whole experience from failure to success. "On the right side" of life you get in tune with the inexorable flow of good.

Many are they who have suffered through painful illnesses that have defied all curative processes. Like the disciples, they have figuratively "toiled all night" in their quest for healing, possibly employing either or both medical and prayer treatment, but without avail. The story seems to imply that regardless of the experience or the techniques involved or even the fervency of the desire, if you are on the "wrong side" (negative state of consciousness) there is no help. The need is to get on the "right side," to get into the flow of the healing stream.

Let's take a look at this healing stream, this universal flow of wholeness. In the previous chapter, we referred to Jesus' command to "consider the lilies of the field, how they grow." Certainly a flower beautifully demonstrates the unobstructed flow of the universe. And in the same sense, though we may not at all be conscious of it, each of us is a flowering of the universal creative process. Each of us is a flow of wholeness. Each of us is whole wherever we are, and whatever may be the conditions of mind or body, because of what Teilhard de Chardin calls "the unimpeachable wholeness of the universe."

You are a child of the universe. You do not walk your path of life alone. The whole universe walks with you. It is dynamically involved in you. Its dynamic flow is ever expressing as you. Thus health is not something you can "get" physically, in pills or potions, or metaphysically in prayers or treatments. You cannot get health. You can only *be* health. Health is the reality of life, the normal condition of man.

The paradox of medical science is that its basic study of "life" has long been done in the laboratory on cadavers. How can one come to know the dynamics of life by studying about death? Little wonder that medicine has insisted that death is the ultimate and sickness is its inevitable prelude to which we must all learn to adjust.

Fortunately there are some hopeful signs. For instance, Cornell University Medical School some years ago decided to research "what makes healthy people healthy." This led the researchers away from the "norm" of deterioration and death and into a study of "healthy-mindedness" as the obvious key to bodily health. The scientists found that the healthiest people are those who have habitual attitudes that make them impervious to social situations and surroundings. Perhaps the time has come when all practitioners in the field of health care will need to agree that health and continuing life are the normal condition of humankind, rather than sickness and death. It might also be refreshing to see a modern application of the ageless Chinese practice in which one pays one's physician to keep him or her well and stops payment when he or she is ill. Certainly it would change the perspective of the doctor and the patient!

Once you catch the idea that you are a whole creature, a child of the universe, the very self-livingness of a universal stream of life, you will never again be satisfied until you find improvement in health. Unity co-founder, Myrtle Fillmore, was a Methodist-bred schoolteacher facing what was in that day a terminal case of tuberculosis. The doctors agreed that she had but a few months to live. It was a condition that had "run in the family," and thus the prognosis was accepted with resignation. She was, however, a spiritual adventurer on the quest for the truth about life. One day she had a great revelation that changed her life, and by her influence, the lives of thousands of people. She affirmed: *I am a child of God and therefore I do not inherit sickness.* She began to cast the net on the right side of the boat. Despite the medical verdict, she got into the flow of healing life and went on to live a full life for forty-five years beyond that time.

This is not to say that heredity has no influence on the conditions or tendencies of the body. But it does say that regardless of the kind of physical body heredity has given you or the conditions of consciousness your parents may have imposed upon you, all this is incidental to your experience of life. Fundamental, however, is the truth that you are a child of the universe. You are in the ceaseless flow of transcendent life. Jesus made it very clear that "it is not the will of my Father . . . that one of these little ones should perish" (Mt. 18:14). He also said, "Come, O blessed of my Father, inherit the kingdom prepared for you from the foundation of the world" (Mt. 25:34). This kingdom in you is the flow of the universe in focus as you. The inheritance is yours, for you are the living enterprise of the creative process. But you must claim it, know that you are entitled to the fullness of life and get into the flow.

God is a circle that is centered in you. All the attributes of the Infinite are in focus as you, flowing forth through you. You are in this flow. You are this flow at the point where you are. Thus you are a child of the universe, a son of God. Meditate on this tremendous insight. It means that you are created in the image-likeness of an infinite idea. You are the only begotten of God from the standpoint that, no matter what other influences may have left their marks on you from the outside, there is that of you that is begotten only of God, which is forever the "flowering" of the divine flow from the inside. This is the fundamental Truth. All else are incidental facts.

The preacher of Ecclesiastes says, "Behold, this alone I found, that God made man upright, but they have sought out many devices" (Eccles. 7:29). Humankind is created in and of a perfect plan of life. And on the right side of the boat, or in the right state of consciousness, humankind will flow with this natural healing stream. But, as Paul says, "For this cause many are weak and sickly among you" (1 Cor. 11:30 KJV). Fishing on the wrong side of the boat, engaging in self-limiting states of mind, we restrict the flow.

We might turn to the story of the fishermen again and note that the fish were there, as always. The change from discouraging emptiness to joyous fulfillment was not in the habits of the fish, but in the attitudes of the fishermen. The healing stream is an eternal reality. There is an allness even within the illness. The whole universe is within you, and its flow is ever the reality *of* you in a fundamental sense, no matter what the incidentals may be. And it is this reality of wholeness that is the key to the constancy of a healing and renewing process within the body—even when you do nothing or know nothing about it.

Some years ago there was a widely published news item telling of the conclusions reached by a former professor at Harvard Medical School. He pointed out that most illnesses are cured without the victims ever knowing they have had them. He cited many instances in which postmortem examinations revealed unmistakable traces of diseases which the subject had conquered without knowing it. He insisted that the body has a superwisdom that is biased in favor of life rather than death and which is ten times as powerful as medicine's imitation. He unblushingly identified this healing power as "God." And then he made a plea that the medical profession inform patients of this great force working within them. He said, "It does the medical profession no good to avoid the word *God*. Why not teach the people the Truth?"

Yes, we need to know the basic Truth that every physiologist accepts without question, that in all life there is an inexorable flow toward wholeness. It is usually called the *vismedicatrix naturae*, which simply means "the healing power of nature." There is a universal tendency for everything to return to normal whenever the balance of life has been violated. Scar a tree with an axe and return after a time, and you will find that nature has healed the scar. Or if you cut your finger peeling potatoes, you may bind the wound, but in two or three days the cut is healed. Medical doctors with all their skills cannot alter this process, and if they are perceptive of the transcendent flow of life, they will say, "I bind the wound, but God heals the cut."

This leads to an important observation of the healing process. Practitioners in any branch of the healing arts are, after all, human. Thus the need for ego-fulfillment sometimes leads them to claim the credit for seemingly miraculous results. However, a doctor is not a healer nor is the "faith healer" or metaphysical practitioner. The healing stream of life is the reality behind every appearance. Whether the method employed is medication or meditation, one can only cooperate in opening the mind or body processes to the ceaseless flow of the healing stream.

The healing stream as a basic flow of life has been dramatically demonstrated in a biological laboratory experiment seeking to prove the "field theory of life." Tree mold was selected as the most unspecialized form of living structure. A slice of the mold was put under a powerful microscope where the viewer could see a lacing of capillarylike rivulets flowing with some form of subcellular fluid. It was discovered that the flow continues for exactly fifty-eight seconds with all the channels flowing in the same direction. Then the flow abruptly halts and reverses itself to flow exactly fifty-eight seconds the other way. There is no known explanation for this phenomenon, but on and on it goes: fifty-eight seconds one way, fifty-eight seconds the other. Back and forth. Perhaps it is the rhythm of the universe.

A metronomic device was developed and carefully synchronized with the fluctuation. Then, with the metronome keeping up the original meter, the tree mold was anesthetized, stopping the flow completely. There was total inactivity of the substance, while the metronome continued its beat. Gradually the anesthesia wore off and the flow in the rivulets resumed, picking up the original beat as indicated by the metronome. This would indicate dramatically that the flow was being directed by a stream of life that is totally transcendent to the life of the tree mold, which had been "out of it."

This would tend to indicate that the beat of the heart, the flow of the blood stream, and the regulation of bodily fluids may well follow the rhythm of a transcendental conductor. Dr. Donald Hatch Andrews calls it the "symphony of life."

The important thing to realize from this experiment is that there is a flow involved even within the inactivated substance. This is the great miracle of life—the key to all healing. Through this fundamental principle and process it can be confidently stated of any person, no matter what the condition, "You can be healed." The means employed may be many and varied, but the reason for the healing is one: the unimpeachable wholeness of the universe. You *can* be healed because you *are* whole! The incidental facts may limit your judgment and your faith, but the fundamental Truth remains: You are a child of the universe, and spiritually, you can never be cut off from the stream of life.

It is an axiom of modern medicine that the only disease is "congestion" and that all other ailments are but an intensification of that congestion which inhibits the natural flow of the healing stream. All congestion first takes root in the mind. Jesus called it *resistance*. Modern researchers may call it *stress*.

A fundamental in electronics is Ohm's law, which says: $C = E \div R$. (Current at the point of use is equal to the power at the source divided by the resistance of the conduit through which it flows.) Even the best conductors offer some resistance, and you can't deliver current without a conductor of some sort. Consider an electric heating or cooking unit. Current flows through wires (normally copper because they are good conductors with little resistance) to a central coil, made of a special alloy that purposely resists the electricity. The result? The resistance to the flow converts the current into heat. An electric light bulb follows the same process, except that the incandescent filament gets "white hot" and converts the current into light.

Now see the relationship of this to the physical body as the channel through which the healing stream (or current of life) flows. Resistance begins in the mind, where self-limiting attitudes become poor conductors for the flow. Then the cells of the body, taking their cue from the mental state, begin to experience resistance and congestion. The result: The healing stream of life is converted into fever and pain and progressive deterioration. Of course, this is an extreme oversimplification, but it indicates how the limitation of consciousness produces stress, which in turn gives rise to all the ills experienced by the physical body.

One common complaint relative to illness is lack of energy—the sense of being tired all the time. Fatigue is a fact that is incidental to the experience of life. But the fundamental Truth is that there is never a shortage of energy, even when you are tired. The physical system is amazing in its ability to mobilize energy by letting the healing stream flow. Watch athletes who are momentarily exhausted from a peak competitive performance. They may throw themselves on the ground, and in a short time will recover their strength. Soon they are back in the competition with renewed strength.

This is reminiscent of that great thought of Isaiah 40:31: "But they who wait for the Lord shall renew their strength, they shall mount up with wings like eagles, they shall run and not be weary, they shall walk and not faint." The word *wait* comes from the Hebrew *qavah* (kawvaw), which literally means "to bind together." It is essentially the same meaning as the root word for *religion,* that which binds or unites man with God. To wait on the Lord, then, means to get in tune, to become one, to get into the flow. It may be summed up in the affirmation: *Be still and know . . . I am in the flow.*

Nine-tenths of all fatigue (in healthy persons) is due to psychological and not physiological factors: financial worries, unsatisfactory working conditions, meaninglessness in life, emotional upsets at home and in business, fear of losing one's job, and so on. Energy, a veritable Niagara of it, is in you constantly, dammed up by forces of which you may be unaware. You may know the Truth, "wait on the

Lord," remove the barriers, get into the flow, and release such stores of energy as will astound you.

Obviously there is much to be said for proper nutrition and exercise in creating and sustaining a healthy balance of the physical system. However, it is significant that Jesus said, "Man shall not live by bread alone, but by every word that proceeds from the mouth of God" (Mt. 4:4). This living word of God is the "healing stream" that flows in and through everyone. The body has an amazing ability to adapt foodstuffs for its needs and to effect what are actual transmutations by the simple act of faith.

Your body is the temple of the living God. It is fed, vitalized, and sustained by the healing and renewing stream of life. If you keep consciously in the flow, you will be guided to eat those things that the body requires. Your tastes will change so that you will begin to desire what you need and not just that which titillates the palate. You will also find unfolding in your natural eating habits a Spirit-motivated diet. "On the right side of the boat," your weight will be normalized, your food will be easily digested, assimilated, and eliminated, and you will come to the freeing experience of eating to live instead of living to eat.

Jesus claimed that more important than what goes into the mouth is what comes out of it. Perhaps He was being facetious. In a more contemporary idiom, He might have said, "Before you have the first cup of coffee in the morning, take time to establish yourself consciously in the flow of life." During the sleep of night, you may have experienced a restoration of energy and a new perspective for the new day. But you will soon be facing the challenges of the marketplace. You will need to know consciously that you are in the flow.

Take a few moments in bed, even before you are up and at it, to "wait on the Lord" or get yourself plugged in. The current of life is within you as always, but you need to get your thoughts consciously on the right side. You can affirm something like this: *I am in the flow of life, and I move easily with the flow. I am radiantly and enthusiastically alive. I am free from tension, stress, and strain, and I go forward in the flow of life—unhurried and unworried.*

Then determine that you will fish only on the right side of the boat. Keep yourself free from negative reactions and the sense of burdensome competition. Your life is to be lived from the inside-out. The things that happen around you or to you can have little bearing on your physical well-being. What counts are the things that happen *in* you. In the East it is said, "You may not be able to keep the birds from flying over your head, but you can keep them from building nests in your hair." When you are in the right consciousness, it will be a case of "none of these things move me." You will be consciously in the flow.

The first crisis of the day will come when someone asks, "How are you?" or "How do you feel?" Now you have a choice: (1) "Incidentally, I feel terrible; my back aches, my stomach is upset, I have a fever, and so on." or (2) "Fundamentally, I am in the flow of life; I am wonderful." The negative response, factual as it may be, will tend to perpetuate that state of consciousness and give rise to continual stress-producing attitudes and the corresponding physical congestion, pain, and deterioration.

Emerson says to gird yourselves about with incessant affirmatives. The reason is easy to see. In this way, you lift the focus from emptiness to fullness, you turn to the other side of the boat, and you actually tend to alter your level of consciousness. And you are not being untruthful, for you are *always* in the flow, and you are always full of wonder because of the "unimpeachable wholeness of the universe."

The moment you start working from the right side you realize that your health is "now here." You can say with confidence: *I am now full of life and health.* The short step from "nowhere" to "now here" is the pause to *be still and know . . . I am in the flow.*

Whenever you have a health problem, remember, *health is now here.* The most important factor in healing is getting out of the "nowhere" consciousness. On this level, the healing effort is motivated by fear and frustrated by the tension of the very anxious effort to find health. Always the first step should be to get into the flow. Life is whole, and you can never be less than whole in the reality of you. Paul says: "We know in part .... But when that which is perfect is come [in consciousness], then that which is in part shall be done away" (1 Cor. 13:9-10 KJV). Get this idea established in consciousness. Affirm: *I am a child of the universe, established eternally in the healing stream. I am strengthened, renewed, restored, and made whole in every way.*

Keep in mind that the healing stream is constant—not present only when you affirm that it is working. You are in this stream constantly, even if you have been fishing on the wrong side of the boat and manifesting less than wellness in experience. The need is not to overcome illness but simply to get into the flow. Any attempt to "overcome" the physical problem may well give rise to even further tension and stress, which will set up conditions that could neutralize your efforts or even make you worse.

There is a healing stream. It is one of the great realities of life. Wherever there is even a faint glimmer of life, that stream is a reality and a potential for help and healing. The question may be asked, "Is it possible for this condition to be healed?" Who can answer? For the condition is a fixation in the consciousness of the person. Let us ask another question, "Is it possible for a structure of great weight to be held to earth by the force of gravity?" Of course it is possible—and inevitable—for gravity is an inexorable force.

There is no incurable illness—only incurable persons who may be locked into certain negative states of consciousness. But consciousness can be changed. One should not oversimplify the process nor assume that by saying a few affirmations or metaphysical treatments a miracle of renewal will easily come. However, know the Truth: *You can be healed; you can open the way to the eternal flow of life.*

> Flow, flow, river of healing,
> Blessing greater than wealth.
> Flow, flow, cleansing, revealing
> God's gift, freedom in health.
> —From an old hymn

CHAPTER 3

The Reality
of
Affluence

In a time when the world is facing the grim specter of lack, there is a great need to understand the omnipresence of divine substance. There is little question that people can fail and even go hungry in their experience of life. But the great truth of the "reality of affluence" is that there is a legitimate abundance for every person, which one can and must claim for oneself, and that lack of any kind in the human experience is the result of some kind of obstruction of the free flow of the creative process.

Lao-tzu was teaching this concept of the flow 3000 years ago. He declared that the human spirit has its source in a cosmic flow, even as rivers have their source in some far-off fountain. To find one's fountain, he said, is to learn the secret of heaven and Earth. Life asks of you only that you flow with it, that you do not resist its inexorable bubbling forth, and that you do not crawl into dark corners of insufficiency and erect barriers. Thus the secret of prosperity and success is that it comes through you and not just to you.

Of course, this contradicts the "wisdom of the world" that has asked: Do you want to earn money, make a living, achieve security, and gain fame and fortune? It is all to be had "out there" in the market place. Of course, you soon learn that a lot of other people are frantically reaching out there for the same plums. You may even experience pressures of competition and the limiting view that another's success is your failure, another's gain is your loss.

This is why Emerson insists that you must "unlearn the wisdom of the world," for it deals with that which is apparent, but not real. "Judge not according to the appearance, but judge righteous judgment" said Jesus (Jn. 7:24 KJV). It would appear that prosperity is simply a matter of having money. But the Truth is that it is being in the flow of substance.

What is money? Pieces of paper and coins of gold are of no value in themselves. Their worth is symbolic of an activity of faith. When persons or organizations have faith in one another, they invest a valuation in various media of exchange. Problems arise when they confuse the symbolic with the real. This is why Paul says, "The love of money is the root of all evils" (1 Tim. 6:10). Not that there is anything intrinsically bad about money, but that we imbue the money with bad vibrations when we work for the symbols rather than for the flow of God or universal substance.

Prosperity is not just having a lot of money. It is having a consciousness of the flow of substance. The true "prosperity consciousness" is consistently open to the flow, attracts opportunities both to give and receive, wisely directs the use of substance, and remains free from its burden. An important guideline: If you are worried about the money you have or don't have, you are out of the flow.

What is success? We have unfortunately equated it with positions and accumulations. We have thought that success comes at a particular rung of the ladder or with the acclaim of the world. This is a delusion. Success is not just "getting there." It is earning the right *to be there*. It is being in the flow of the creative process.

The drive for success is basic in the American dream. In our cherished idealism, anyone can reach the top of the heap. Unfortunately, this has given rise to the feeling that everyone should want to do so, and to the judgment that anything short of "success" is failure. The paradox is that in a culture that is almost totally success-oriented, there is a pervasive consciousness of failure. For, how much room is there at the top? This is what we may call the "success syndrome."

For instance, those who may otherwise lead a life of creativity and meaning are almost ashamed to admit that they have been in the same job for twenty years. People think, and sometimes say,

"Are you still on that job? What's the matter with you?" True, they may lack ambition. But it could be that they are where they are because they are secure in what they are. They may have made a conscious decision many times over to resist the pressures of conformity to the common search for the "Holy Grail" of material success, giving priority to quality in the kind of work they do and the kind of life they live with their families.

Spurred on by the "success syndrome," many persons set their sights on making a lot of money. There are only two ways to "make money": (1) to work at the U.S. Mint, or (2) to become a counterfeiter. The urge to make money is a basic human response to the acquisitive instinct, but it is a sure way to get out of the flow of universal substance. We may succeed in papering our self-image with a painted-on opulence and building our life around a stagnant pool of materialism, but in terms of the fullness of life, we are out of the flow. This may be why Solomon said, "With all thy getting get understanding" (Prov. 4:7 KJV).

One of the great fundamentals of the "flow of life" is the *reality of affluence*. The word *affluence* is normally used in the context of things: houses, cars, money—materiality in general. This is actually a corruption of the true meaning of the word. It means "flow forth," or "the free flow." The same corruption is found in the use of the word *currency*. We use the term in reference to money in bundles or in accounts. But currency implies a flow. Certainly money has no power except in its use.

When you get into the consciousness of the flow of the creative process within you, there will be a constant inner-direction in your life, leading to a deep sense of meaning, and incidentally, as it flows forth, leading to the cars, houses, and money that are part of this meaning—but with none of them becoming the goal of life and all of them a joyous experience in its free flow.

This is strongly implied in the teachings of Jesus, though it is generally obscured through a failure to understand the within-out process that He articulated. He said, "But seek ye first the [His] kingdom . . . and all these things shall be added unto you" (Mt. 6:33 KJV). He is not talking about a place in space but a depth in consciousness. The kingdom of God is the universal flow within you. It is the one great reality behind every appearance.

Place yourself in the middle of the stream, says Emerson, and you will be impelled without effort to a "right and perfect contentment." This stream of life is the only reality. Knowing that you are in the flow of this stream is the basis for faith and the key to the only kind of security you can ever know. And this stream that flows from within you has no other intent except to flow through you and as you. This is why Jesus said that it is the Father's good pleasure to give you the kingdom.

There is no room in this new insight for the old belief that God wills lack or limitation or that it is a grace to be poor. The beatitude says: "Blessed are the poor in spirit, for theirs is the kingdom of heaven" (Mt. 5:3). The implication has been given that people are blessed in their poverty, for they will have their reward in some future experience in some far-off place of golden streets. This is totally inconsistent with the dynamics of Jesus' teaching.

"Poor in spirit" means "poor in pride" or rich in an attitude of humility. It means to let go the ego and the willful determination to *have* something without first *being* something. To be poor in spirit means to be open and receptive to the flow of good from within-out. And the promise is: "Yours is the kingdom of heaven." You will give birth to the unborn possibility of limitless substance that is forever within you.

"The practice of the presence of God" is an insight that has been inspiring to many. However, its full implication is rarely caught or taught. The presence of God is the activity of God that is *present* in you and *as* you. Thus to practice the Presence means to practice thinking that you are surrounded by a divine Presence that wishes you well because you are expressing its life. The flow of life is the very nature of God and the natural experience of humankind. In the last chapter, we dealt with the idea that health is the natural expression of life and that it is not natural to be sick in any form. In the same way, affluence, or the free flow of substance, is the natural state of things for you. It is unnatural for you to experience lack or limitation in any way at any time. Charles Fillmore put it bluntly, "It is a sin to be poor."

It is a full circle from the "grace of poverty" to this new insight that lack is a sin. Fillmore did not imply a judgment of the segment of society that lives below the "poverty level." The word *sin* must be seen here in the context of Lao-tzu's thought that "anything is evil that blocks the flow of creative action, and everything is healthy that flows with the universe." Sin is more than just acts or experiences of limitation. It is the frustration of the God-process that gives rise to them. Wherever there is lack of any kind, there must be a frustration of the flow of abundance. Until this fundamental is realized and corrective measures employed, all the poverty programs in the world will not really change things in society.

You are not created outside the universe. You are an integral part of it, a dynamic center within it. The allness of universal substance is forever moving into and through the "eachness" that you are. This creative flow has produced you, and you belong to and in it in a more vital sense than it belongs to you. It is not just that you inherit it. You are its expression. The free flow of substance within you is the continuation of the divine effort that made you in the first place.

You may be inclined to judge the conditions of your life on the basis of the stock market performance, the rate of inflation, or the possibilities of employment. This tendency and all the "facts" that are accumulated through it must be "unlearned." You must learn to "judge righteous judgment," to get the transcendent perception of life in a dynamic universe. As one man wisely said, "Many times I have been broke, but I have never been poor." The economy may fluctuate in recessions and depressions, but you can never be cut off from the all-sufficient substance of Spirit. Prosperity is, thus, the law of the universe and not just a condition of the fortunate.

Paul says, "And my God will supply every need of yours according to his riches" (Phil. 4:19). Every need! It is a fantastic promise! Note, however, that he does not say that God will fill your lack. A *need* is a vessel to be filled, while *lack* is a state of mind, a limitation of consciousness. Hold a cup under an open faucet and it is quickly filled. However, this process would be completely frustrated if the cup were to be held under the flow of water upside down.

Could this be what the Psalmist had in mind when he sang, "My cup runneth over"? Perhaps it is not just the joyous realization of "things going great." Maybe it is a statement of the process involved in good times and bad. Since "it is your Father's good pleasure to give you the kingdom," your cup is always running over. You are always in the flow of affluence, but sometimes you may inadvertently frustrate the flow by a mind stayed on negation and self-limitation.

This may well be the "unforgivable sin": the mind that is made up. If you have a conviction that your life is empty, that you have been discriminated against, that you have never had a chance in the "mainstream of life," then your cup is running over—right over the bottom side of an upsidedown vessel. The sin is unforgivable in the sense that no one can alter the situation except the one who is blocking the flow. You may pray and treat for prosperity, but until you get consciously and receptively into the flow, there will be no change.

You may feel justified in your worry and fear over financial problems or in your resistance and resentment toward persons or forces that appear to be keeping your good from you. But the plain truth is the free flow of substance is being dammed up from within, and not without. This is why Jesus said, "Agree with thine adversary quickly" (Mt. 5:25 KJV). The adversary is not the competition or personal antagonist "out there." It is your negative or adverse thought about them. No one can keep your good from you but you.

When you are consciously in the flow, you solve one of the great problems of life: You feel a constancy of the creative process flowing in and through you, and thus there is no feeling of fear, anxiety, or insecurity. Remember, Jesus said we should not be anxious about what we should eat or wear, but we should work for the awareness that we are in the flow in which all will be taken care of. Holding on in fear or strain or anxiety out of a sense of personal insufficiency is as effective a frustration of flow as if you stepped firmly on the garden hose. To "let go" does not imply unconcern or immature irresponsibility. It is a willingness to let the law work. Cast the burden on the Lord! Stop worrying and start believing!

Emerson had this consciousness of the flow of life which indwells each person as a Presence and which is forever bubbling forth through each person as a fountain. He insists that, if you do not have your share, it is actually rushing to meet you, following you like a shadow.

One of the ways to make such a concept practical is in connection with your work. If you are looking for a job, get the feeling that someone is looking for you. Affirm that there is a right place for you and that you are guided in all your ways of locating it.

It is vitally important to carefully analyze your attitudes toward your work. If you think of work as a place to make money or to make a living, you are out of the flow of life. You are contradicting the fundamental principle that life is lived from within-out. Work not to make a living but to make a life. Most job dissatisfaction springs from the tendency to emphasize what work does for you instead of what flows through you while you work.

Emerson insists that no matter what your work may be, let it be your own. No matter what your occupation, let what you are doing be "organic"; let it be in your bones. He says that in this way you open the door for the affluence of heaven and Earth to stream through you.

All work is an opportunity by which you can get into the flow of life. It doesn't matter what the nature of the work may be. What counts is the attitude with which you approach it. The support of the universe is constant in you, and the creative process is constantly seeking to flow forth through you. Meditate on this Truth as you sit at your desk (or bench or sales counter) in the morning. Don't even joke about "another day, another dollar." You work, and you are paid for the work. But if that is all that is experienced, you will always be underpaid and unfulfilled.

When a bolt of lightning flashes in the sky and crashes into a tree, you are experiencing an illusion. What the eye does not see is the tiny "leader bolt" of energy that shoots down to make contact with the tree. The massive charge that lights up the sky is the great voltage of the Earth's mass flowing up that tiny bolt into the clouds. It is not the lightning from the sky that strikes and destroys the tree but the tremendous charge that flows from within the tree itself.

Think of this in terms of your work. It would appear that your job is the means of attracting money from the world. And of course it is, but there is so much more involved. You are a focus of the affluence of heaven and Earth. The work is the contact by which a flow may unfold. The need is to "practice the Presence" of this inner flow. Meditate on the ideal that the creative process of the universe is rushing, streaming, pouring into you from all sides while you do your work. Get this feeling so strongly that your whole being bubbles with enthusiasm and your fingers tingle with power. Working in this consciousness, you are in the flow of life. Your work will be done effectively, but without ego. And because there is a true spirit of giving, there will be a fulfilling demonstration of receiving.

If you need work or if you need improvement in your work or new directions in your career, "practice the Presence" of this creative flow in you. Know that you are an instrument of creative potentiality seeking only to discover a contact by which to release the flow. The mentality will be on the level of "give" instead of "get." You will draw to you or be drawn toward the kind of work opportunities where you can be both blessed and a blessing. And in that kind of contract, there is always a manifestation of prosperity and success.

"Opportunity knocks only once!" How often we have heard this old saw! It is one of the many axioms of the "wisdom of the world" that must be unlearned, for it is completely untrue. It is a principle in nature that there is a ceaseless flow of the infinite process within every person. Revelation 3:20 puts it symbolically: "Behold, I stand at the door and knock; if any one hears my voice and opens the door, I will come in to him and eat with him, and he with me." Thus, the truth is, opportunity knocks constantly. It is as if you were living in a country where any place you drilled for oil you would bring in a gusher. The inner flow of Spirit is constant, and thus any kind of lack or failure must be accounted for through the frustration of the flow in consciousness. *And consciousness can be changed!*

Malachi 3:10 KJV puts it in the clearest possible way: "Prove me now herewith . . . if I will not open you the windows of heaven, and pour you out a blessing, that there shall not be room enough to receive it." In the traditional view of heaven "up there," this would seem to say that God will fill your life with divine "goodies." Obviously there is a deeper and more relevant meaning.

Heaven is within you, the very focus of the flow of the Infinite upon you. Thus we need to look again at the inner meaning of Malachi. "Prove me" means "get in tune with the flow." "I will open you, the windows of heaven." The insertion of a comma gives a new implication. You are the windows of heaven. You are the open channel for the flow. "I

59

will . . . pour *you* out a blessing." You become a blessing of life and creativity and success. "There shall not be room enough to receive it" indicates that you are suddenly blessed with more opportunities than you can possibly handle. Life is rich and full, because you are consciously centered in the flow of life.

Here is a good realization on which to practice the Presence: *Opportunity is wherever I am! I am in the flow, and every day I expect new things to happen that will open the way to success. I put my whole self into everything that I do and pour myself out as a blessing wherever I go.*

It is a great thing to realize that the free flow of the Infinite in you is limitless. Your mind is not just a limited vessel of awareness that may occasionally be enriched by some flash of divine inspiration. There is only one Mind, and your mind is a state of consciousness within Divine Mind. Ideas are the "currency" of mind and are convertible and converted into money and the innovations that attract it. Because you live within the allness of God-Mind, you are always in the flow of creative and success-producing ideas. There is never a limit to the flow, only a belief in limitation which restricts it.

The story is told of Dave Brubeck, the master improvisational jazz musician, and his bout with fear. For years he has played concerts all over the world, night after night, with no score and no preplan. Just a continuous flow of creativity and improvisations and modulations, never repeating, always new and different and exciting.

One night, driving with some of his band in a snowstorm, he began to think about the "drain" of creativity. There was a brief period when he was chilled with the fear that one night he would suddenly run dry—no ideas, no melodies, no rhythms. Since this was his whole stock in trade, it was a shattering experience for a few moments. The windshield wiper began to struggle in its effort to sweep away the accumulation of heavy snow. And there was his answer. For he recalled that in all the world and through all time, snow had been falling somewhere, and yet no two snowflakes had ever been identical. How could the creative flow, upon which he depended so much, ever run dry in him? The fear was gone, never to return.

Yes, God will supply every need if we open our minds in an enthusiastic desire to give. Ideas, plans, and forms will come easily and flow freely, putting words in our mouths, directing our hands, and moving our feet in the way we should go. All that is required is that we keep in the flow, keep open in mind and heart by positive thoughts and creative faith, and that we keep moving "in the direction of our dreams."

This recalls the lesson of Henry David Thoreau, the philosopher-dreamer, who went to the woods to experience the aliveness of being in the flow. I return to *Walden* occasionally, for he has so much to say that is relevant to my need for understanding of myself and of life. He sums up his *Walden* experience by saying that if we advance confidently in the direction of our dreams and get into the flow of universal laws, we will come to live with the "license of a higher order of beings." And maybe, just maybe, this is how Jesus was able to walk on water. But certainly, and some would call it an even greater miracle, when we are consciously in the flow of life, we will live with the license to alter our lives.

Not that you can or should become better than another person or even good enough to fulfill certain worldly standards. This is giving too much power to the world "out there." In the wisdom of the East there is an axiom that says: *There is nothing noble about being superior to some other person. True nobility is being superior to your previous self.* When you get into the consciousness of the ceaseless flow of life, you open the way for continued growth and betterment.

Affluence, in terms of the free flow of ideas, substance, and creativity, is the one reality of life. As you increasingly know this Truth and identify with it, there will be a steady improvement of your position in the world. In the flow of life, you are in tune with the wealth of the universe, which is yours to share. "Come, O blessed of my Father, inherit the kingdom prepared for you from the foundation of the world" (Mt. 25:34).

CHAPTER 4

The Effusion
of
Light

We are living today in a complex and changing world. If there is one thing one needs more than anything else, it is light: light in terms of insight into self, guidance along life's way, knowledge of the secrets of the universe, and the wisdom to use light and not abuse it. The clearest thinkers the race has produced have always seen the course of their lives as the quest for light. It is said that Goethe, who spent his life on this quest, gasped the last words on his deathbed: "More light!"[1]

And yet invariably the search has been "out there." We have thought of light in terms of ideas and innovations, or the minds that gave birth to them. His followers saw Jesus as *the* light, instead of one who gave evidence of "the true light that enlightens every man . . . coming into the world" (Jn. 1:9). It is true that He said, "I am the light of the world." But He also said, "You are the light of the world.... Let your light so shine" (Mt. 5:14,16).

Light is the reality of God within all creation. It is the reality of our own potential. All overcoming, all healing, all self-expansion is the inevitable effect of the dawning of light within and its effusion without. It is of this that Isaiah speaks: "Then shall thy light break forth as the morning, and thine health shall spring forth speedily" (Is. 58:8 KJV).

Humankind forever stands at the crossroads of human experience, and the darkness of fear and indecision is overwhelming. Which way to go? What to choose? Who or what to vote for? One of the chief causes of strain is living in the awareness that even little decisions can influence our whole lives. Who of us cannot identify with Robert Frost as he muses:

> Two roads diverged in a wood, and I—
> I took the one less traveled by,
> And that has made all the difference.[2]

From the earliest times humankind has yearned for some way to see beyond the horizon and thus to know the ultimate course of those "two roads." The precursors of religion are the medicine men and fortune-tellers and seers and prophets who were able, or claimed they were, to look into the future. The very word *Providence*, long used as a synonym for God, comes from root words that mean "to see forward." And the dictionary definition of the word *religion* is "divine revelation for human guidance."

Humankind has instinctively sensed a dimension of life in which there flows, like an underground stream, a directive force that is forever correspondent with every conscious need. Emerson talks of this:

> There is guidance for each of us, and by lowly listening we shall hear the right word. Why need you choose so painfully? . . . Certainly there is a possible right for you that precludes the need of . . . wilful election. For you there is a reality, a fit place .... Place yourself in the middle of the stream of power and wisdom which animates all whom it floats, and you are without effort impelled to truth, to right and a perfect contentment.[3]

This effusion of light is one of the mysteries of nature, where we call it instinct. A salmon, spawned in a certain river, instinctively leaves that river and makes its way to the sea. Then, at the proper time for mating and spawning, it returns, over thousands of trackless miles, to the very river in which it was born. A bird is directed to migrate to a warmer climate, leaving at the precise time, flying in the specific direction, wending its way to a destination it has never seen, and flying unerringly as on a radar beam.

We say, "Isn't nature wonderful?" And thus we quickly dispose of the matter. Paraphrasing Jesus,

"If God so endowed the lesser creatures of life, shall He not much more endow you, O ye of little faith?" If anyone evidences, even in a brief showing, this kind of inner-direction, we call it "extra-sensory perception" or "psychic phenomenon." It is a very subtle put-down, for it tends to deny the inherent flow of guidance in humankind that is just as natural as the instinct in animals.

Mark Twain once told of a time that he had great need of an article that he had written for a magazine many years earlier. He wrote the publishers for it only to be advised that the demand for the particular issue had been so great they did not even have a file copy left. His only copy had gotten away from him. So with great determination, he set out to find a copy. He began by asking friends, but none had it. He said to himself, "I know there is a copy somewhere, and someone knows that he has it. Someday, at sometime, I will run into that person."

Several weeks later he was in New York on business. He was waiting at a traffic light at Fifth Avenue and Forty-second Street. Suddenly, a strange man, one of the thousands who had been passing, accosted him: "Oh, Mr. Twain! This is odd! I was just on my way to the post office to mail you this old magazine. I was cleaning out my files last night and came across it. I found that it contained an article you had written, and since it was published some years ago, it occurred to me that you might like to have it." He handed an envelope to Twain and disappeared into the crowd. It contained the very copy of the magazine that he had been searching for.

There are those who prefer to deal with such occurrences with extreme skepticism. Some would say, "If it happened at all, it must have been pure coincidence!" But the odds favoring such a chance event would be astronomical. Or it is considered a "miracle of God" or an evidence of psychic communication. Why do we refuse to accept as fact that "there is a spirit in man: and the inspiration of the Almighty giveth them understanding" (Job 32:8 KJV)?

A common term in religion is *prayer for guidance*. But it is rare that the prayer seeks a firsthand experience of God, an effusion of light. Normally, it is an attempt to coax a miracle from a reluctant God. More often it is an effort to seek divine approval on something one has already decided to do regardless. How easy it is to "pray for guidance" and then to get an answer supported by a whole array of rationalizations for why we *should* do what we *want* to do. It is a little game we play.

Guidance is not a special act of God or a phenomenon dealing with some exterior force acting upon man. Natural guidance is divine, and divine guidance is natural. Man is a creature of light, thus even if we frustrate it through fear, we are always in the flow of guidance. If we pray to

God "out there" for light and guidance, our prayer may actually block the flow of light and guidance from within. The need is to "lowly listen," to get into the consciousness of the flow. Light is an omnipresent reality. We don't have to reach it, or even reach for it, but to give up the very desire to reach. *Be still and know . . . I am in the flow.*

Light or guidance may but need not come as a voice heard by the ear or as a phenomenon that is seen by the eyes. We may be impressed, for instance, with the story of Paul and his dramatic experience on the Damascus road, assuming that our guidance should come in some such spectacular way. It might come to some persons in this way. However, there is no evidence that it ever came to Jesus in this way.

In his book *Talks With Great Composers,* Arthur Abell quotes Brahms as saying:

> I always contemplate my oneness with the Creator before commencing to compose. I immediately feel vibrations that thrill my whole being ... I see clearly what is obscure in my ordinary moods ... Straightway the idea flows in upon me ... Measure by measure, the finished product is revealed.[4]

"Ah," we say, "but Brahms was a genius!" How we evade all possible intimations of a divine dimension in humankind! The genius does not differ from other persons in his or her access to light—only in his or her confident acceptance of its effusion. As we witness the exploits of the "genius" in music, art, science, or business, we should recall Jesus' idea: "All these things that I do, you can do too ... and greater things than these shall you do." This can happen to us—if we get into the flow.

Walter Russell, artist, scientist, philosopher, insists that the universe does not bestow favors on the few whom it seeks out as interpreters. He says it is just the reverse—the universe gives to those who plug in, mediocrity is self-inflicted and genius is self-bestowed. We should cultivate the silence and when we are alone, the universe will talk to us in flashes of inspiration. Knowledge is ours for the asking. We do not have to learn anything. In fact, all we really need to do is recollect it, for it is already within us as the reality of light.

In education the emphasis is normally placed on the acquisition of knowledge. Thus the better the memory and the more exhaustive the notebooks and files, the higher the grade. However, progressive educators are beginning to realize, as did the ancient Greeks, that true education is the process of waking up to life and releasing the effusion of light. If we want to get the most from our human potential, we must realize that it is entirely sensible, scientific, and logical to permit the effusion of universal light to direct the conscious mind. The

director of research of a large corporation challenges college engineering students to be alert to
hunches, to keep the mind open. He discourages
too much reliance on logic and urges students to
make a concerted effort to locate the treasure
chest of ideas that lies hidden within the individual.

When we complete our education, we are ready
as an instrument; but until we learn to open the
vertical dimension of the mind, we are only half a
person, and half the person we can be. Harvard
poet-philosopher George Santayana insists that it
is not wisdom to be only wise and to close the eyes
to the inward flow. He says it is wisdom to believe
the heart and to trust the "soul's invincible sur-
mise."

What is called "divine guidance" is a flow of
Infinite Mind. It is universal in that it is a principle
of mind action and not dependent upon a special
appeal. It is personal in that it is a process of the
presence of this Mind that "knows what you need
before you ask him" (Mt. 6:8). It makes no choice
for you, but it is the urge and energy through which
you can make the choice that is best in terms of
your own consciousness. It is not a special act of
God but a specialization of the omniscience and
omni-action of the presence of God.

Divine guidance is not prejudiced. It does not
come with one fixed and unalterable step to be
taken. It is, rather, a wisdom, a light, a supportive
flow that enables you to see the road ahead with

amazing clarity and to use your own wisdom at its highest level of development. Divine guidance can never lead you to take a step that is beyond your ability to understand or rightly use.

Some persons puzzle over the question, "How can one distinguish between divine guidance and human will?" The very question implies a duality—a sense of God "out there" who would or could desire for you something contrary to your personal desires. Divine guidance is not an exterior force acting upon you. It is the seed of your divinity (the Christ of you) seeking to fulfill its pattern in the outforming process of your life. God could never want for you that which you do not inherently want for yourself.

Of course, willfulness can be a problem. But then the first step in prayer is to let go the ego, to give consent to the flow of the "unimpeachable wholeness of the universe." You may not succeed on every occasion in letting the flow of your own pattern have its way. This is why the term *practice the Presence* is so meaningful. Paul advises us to "study to shew thyself approved unto God" (2 Tim. 2:15 KJV). This does not mean trying to win divine approval. You are always as approved of God as you are of sunlight. Your work is to determine how you are blocking the flow. Then open the windows, step out of the shadows into the light. And this may take effort and perseverance.

"How do you get to Mt. Olympus?" a man once

asked of Socrates. He replied, "Just make every step you take go in that direction." In more recent times, a man stopped Heifetz on the streets of New York and asked, "How do you get to Carnegie Hall?" The musical genius replied, "Practice, practice, practice." The watchword could well be: Keep on . . . until you catch on! Study and work and pray . . . until the light comes. Only then can you really know what Jesus had in mind when He said, "You will know the truth, and the truth will make you free."

Light was an important reality to Jesus. Perhaps we do not fully appreciate His teachings or the great experiences of His life until we see the light. We are told "that God is light and in him is no darkness at all" (1 Jn. 1:5). But what is light?

It is possible that we never really see light. We only see what it does to us, or more correctly, what it causes us to do. Is light the white radiance of the light bulb? Is it the intangible essence that is conveyed by electrical energy through the wires? Or could light be an ever-present nonmaterial reality that is simply awakened or released by these forces?

Does light fill space, like air? If I go into a room in the daylight and pull down dark shades over the windows, the light does not escape through any hole, but it is no longer present as air is. Where does light come from? And where does it go? We are told that light joins us from the sun after traveling the ninety-three million miles in eight minutes. But wait. Does a pain travel through space to me from a boy who hits me in the face with a stone? The pain is what happened to me. If the stone had not hit me but had broken a window, the result would have been quite different. All I know is that a force hit me and there was a certain effect on me. The sun sends out force, not light or heat.

So what is light? Obviously, as the Bible talks about it, and perhaps as science talks about it, light is a transcendent thing. Perhaps light is an everywhere-present reality which sometimes, as a result of certain conditions, becomes visible to the eyes. Cells appear to have an innate glow of light. The whole body gives off a kind of light or "aura" which some persons and certain instrumentation can see. Light then, may well be the one great reality of things, beyond appearances.

Cartoonists have long depicted a flash of understanding as a light bulb over the head. When you are consciously in the flow of life, there is an effusion of light that manifests as understanding, as guidance, as creativity. But it is not something that God "out there" sends to you. It is, rather, an expanded awareness of the "true light" in the presence of God that is present in you and *as* you. It is a moment of oneness, a feeling of being centered in God, and of being the center of God. Suddenly there is a creative flow—"Let there be light."

So when Jesus said "let your light shine," He meant let yourself *be* what you really are, or as Eckhart puts it, "let God be God in you." When you are in the flow of life, you become transparent in the sense that the human of you, the ego, the personality, and the flesh and blood body, become an open channel to let the light flow forth as the reality of you.

A couple took their small boy with them to Europe where they visited many of the cathedrals on the tourist trek. On their return home, the boy was in Sunday school when the teacher asked, "What is a saint?" Remembering the many stained-glass cathedral windows depicting the Christian saints, the boy said, "A saint is a man who the light shines through."

Perhaps Emerson had this in mind when he said: "A man is the facade of a temple wherein all wisdom and all good abide. What we commonly call man, the eating, drinking, planting, counting man, does not, as we know him, represent himself, but misrepresents himself."[5] You are more than you think you are, more than you appear to be. You are a window of God through which the light may shine. When you get yourself out of the way, you may experience the effusion of light flowing forth as wisdom and guidance and creativity.

"Earth's crammed with heaven, and every common bush afire with God,"[6] sings Elizabeth Barrett Browning. She is referring to the experience of

Moses who came upon a bush that appeared to be on fire without being consumed. As he approached it to get a better look, he had a flash of inspiration. A voice from within said, "Put off your shoes from your feet, for the place on which you are standing is holy ground" (Ex. 3:5). This is one of the great revelations of all time. Man has a tendency to cast about everywhere for light, for inspiration, for direction. Moses suddenly realized, "I am the burning bush; I am the flaming light of God."

Light is where you are, and it is the complete answer to what you need, now and always. To "take your shoes off" means to let go the false beliefs of consciousness and "lowly listen." The light you seek is not somewhere else, but where you are. Don't ask God to guide you or beg God to make the choice for you. Instead, affirm that you are in the flow of light, and God is the light. You are in it. It is in you. It is the reality of you. It is not something to reach for but a Truth to accept. Know that there is that in you that knows the right and perfect direction for your life and affirm that you are now acting under that guiding light.

You are forever in the flow of guidance. Don't wait to be guided. We are told to "wait on the Lord," but the word *wait* comes from the root word that means "to bind together." This kind of "waiting" implies plugging in to the divine circuits. It is not a question of time but a depth of consciousness. Expect to be guided and then get in motion.

Take a step, choose a course of action. Do what
you can do and go as far as you can go. Guidance
is a process that works most effectively when you
are in motion.

One of the chief causes of stress in life—which
gives rise to all sorts of emotional and physical
ills—is the pressure of making decisions. The very
term *make a decision* implies something that must
be personally put together in the workshop of the
mind. Actually, there is no need, ever, to "make"
a decision. The very effort to "make" the decision
tends to frustrate the spontaneous flow of guidance.

The only decision you have to make is the
decision to begin. The decisions "what to do" and
"which way to go" should not be made; they should
be *discovered*. Life is whole and complete, and
even when you may be seeing it in part, there is
always a right answer "in that stream of power and
wisdom" within. It is that in you that knows beyond
your conscious knowing. If you lowly listen, you
will hear the right word, and the directions will
easily unfold. This doesn't mean doing nothing,
saying, Pollyanna-style, "Oh, it will work out—I
will just wait for an answer." Remember, when you
plug in to a power source or turn on the light
switch, there is no delay in the flow. Be still and
know that you are in the flow and then move with
it.

The term *discover a decision* does not imply

predestination. The only predestiny in life is the ultimate unfoldment of the divine creature you are. But the direction you take in realizing this outforming of the Christ indwelling will always be determined by your consciousness. However, there is a creative intention working in you. It is a force that transcends mistakes and wrong choices and makes all things work for good. It is like an organist who may touch a wrong note and create a dissonance, and who skillfully uses that wrong note as a leading tone by which to modulate into a new key. He makes it appear as if the whole progression was intended that way, as if it were the only way it could have been.

You cannot really make a wrong choice, a bad decision. Any step you take will lead eventually to your good, because a negative experience encountered will produce the challenge in which to outgrow the kind of consciousness from which the choice was made, leading to a higher consciousness from which more constructive steps will be taken. So a wrong choice is a right choice at that particular time. Know this, you are free from the fear of bad decisions. You can stand still and believe that there is no decision to be made, only a direction to discover.

The next time you have an important decision to make, give yourself a chance. Let your mind become an instrument rather than thinking of it as the source. Get plugged in and let this fantastic process work for you. In the end, you will not make the decision; the decision will make you.

Your mind is your kingdom. It has no boundaries. The free flow of ideas and creativity is your inheritance. It is important to begin acting on the belief that you can dip into this process at any time, manifesting guidance and light in creative and imaginative ways that are beyond human knowing. For it is a wellspring that is inexhaustible.

We are told that "in a moment, in the twinkling of an eye" He will come. Traditionalists have insisted that this is the promise of Jesus' return in the flesh. However, Jesus saw Himself not as the great exception but as the great example of the flow of the universal process in man. And if He was the great example, it must be as the example of that which we have it in us to become. And it was to this *becoming* in us and not to His physical return that His statements pertained. This is the "second coming." And it will happen in a flash. And not just once and for all, but any time we are in need of the effusion of light. The inference is that we should not try to make decisions or generate ideas, for this only leads to anxiety and strain. It also leads to information gathering. Thought has never solved the problems of man and never will. Perhaps this is why Jesus says that this awakening (to light) will come "in such an hour as ye think not" (Mt. 24:44 KJV). The more you think about a problem, the more complex and uncertain it becomes, unless and until the light comes. And what is that light? It is the flow of transcendent guidance.

There is light, guidance, inspiration, creativity ever with you, ever within you, as supermind resources. Whenever you face a crisis, in a moment when you think not, there is an answer. Don't think about the problem, rather let the effusion of divine light remold your mind from within. Suddenly the "problem" gives way to the projection of light that leads to the outforming of your good. "In a moment," "in the twinkling of an eye," you can plug in and feel the surge of light. Time is no factor, for there is no time in Spirit. As fast as you can snap your fingers, the answer can come in the form of the completed plan and all the means for its fulfillment.

Creative people—writers, poets, artists, and composers—often have to struggle and strain in arduous labor in formulating some of their works. But there are times when they are in the flow of the creative process and inspiration comes in a flash. Beethoven, we are told, was once sitting in his chair and in one flash he heard, as one great chord, an entire symphony. Today that work requires an hour to perform, and it took him weeks to get it down on paper. But he caught the entire symphony "in the twinkling of an eye."

Get this idea into your consciousness. When you are pressured with time in accomplishing something that may require a flow of inspiration, just snap your fingers lightheartedly, as a symbolic reminder that in one instant the light may come with a complete answer to your need. Not that you should expect everything to be done for you. For nothing is really done *for* you—only through you. The first steps are your own preparation of gathering information. But there is a time when you must let go and open the way for the outformation of the creative flow.

There are not thousands of things to learn in life. There is only one thing to learn: to know the Knower within and to sincerely and regularly "acknowledge Him in all our ways." This is to understand the superconscious level of mind, to learn to think vertically and not just horizontally, to deal with transcendental and not just human logic. How relaxed you can be when you see that the flow of life in you is as natural as the inexorable force of gravity. Wherever you are and whatever may be the urgency of need, you can be still and know that you are in the flow. You will experience an effusion of light in the form of creative ideas, unerring guidance, and answers without ceasing.

CHAPTER 5

The Art
of
Getting Along

Life is set in the framework of human relations. Though conflicts arise between people, human beings are essentially gregarious creatures. Getting along with people is certainly a prerequisite to happiness and security because all humankind is interdependent. But, even more, it is a longing of the heart that arises out of the transcendent awareness of unity. People yearn for "repose in God" because they innately know that they are one in Spirit. And they are restless and uneasy in the face of all human conflict because they sense that beyond the appearance of separation there is an underlying bond of divine love.

Lao-tzu said that one lives in proportion to the number of points with which he or she contacts life and the world, inferring that the flow of life must go outward to form a harmonious interaction with people. One who frustrates this flow by harboring thoughts of resistance, prejudice, or animosity only half lives. This is why Jesus stressed as the great law: "Thou shalt love the Lord thy God with all thy heart ... soul ... mind ... and ... strength ... [and] thy neighbour as thyself" (Mk. 12:30-31 KJV). Not that God will be offended if you do not love God, or that your neighbor, by his or her actions, is always deserving of your love. To love God and your neighbor is to "establish the points" with which you contact life and the world. It is to get into the flow of love. You will invariably find it easier to *get along* with people when you *go along* with the movement of the flow.

Divine order is not simply an ultimate toward which to work through some prayer technique that claims its reality. It is a fundamental Truth of the universe. There is always a cosmos within every chaos. There is always enough love to go around, even within the persons involved in bitter disputes. In the flow of life, there is a potential for peace and understanding and cooperation in every relationship. And as Lao-tzu says, whoever flows as life flows has solved the human equation.

The art of getting along is not a psychological gimmick by which to love the unlovable and communicate with the incommunicable. It is not simply adjusting to or making the best of human perversity. The "getting along" relates only secondarily to the other person. Primarily, it refers to getting along with the reality of your Self and the determination to keep the channels of consciousness free from any and all obstructions.

A woman described an experience on the subway one morning on her way to work. She boarded the car at her station, and seeing an empty seat, walked resolutely toward it. Just as she was about to sit down, another woman, coming from another door, "knocked her flying" in the struggle for the seat. The "victim" turned on the now-seated woman in a rage. She called her an "animal" and other things she later regretted. The whole episode left her in a turmoil of anger at the woman and guilt at her own loss of composure. She said, "But what can I do when someone acts like this? How can I keep myself in the spirit of love and harmony, when everywhere I go I run into this kind of behavior? What is wrong with the world anyway?"

Can you identify with this experience? Instead of a subway, it could be a bus or a conflict with another car while driving. It could be a conflict with someone in your family or neighborhood or a co-worker in your office. Instead of a seat, it could be a promotion or a grant or a coveted prize. So let's think about it as if it were your experience. Jesus said, "What is that to thee? follow thou me" (Jn. 21:22 KJV). This doesn't mean to be blindly indifferent to what goes on in the world around you. But it does mean that before you try to understand or even correct conditions "out there," you need first to get yourself consciously established in the flow of life. It would seem obvious that the other person was out of the flow of love and harmony. But then that is his or her responsibility to live with. The incident is most certainly external, but the reaction is completely your own.

There is a flow of harmony and love every- where, whether you are aware of it or not, and whether you are consciously moving in it or not. This is what the "omnipresence of God" means. You do not leave the presence of God or the flow of life and love when you are negative or resistant. You leave the *consciousness* of the Presence. But you are in the flow and the flow is in you *every* moment and in *every* experience.

You may not know exactly how or why you lose the consciousness and the enveloping experience of the flow, but of one thing you can be sure: if you are being pushed around, you are out of it. You may want to fight back or cry foul. You may be certain that the problem is "out there," but the desire to retaliate or incriminate is a state of *your* consciousness. If, as you charge, the other person is an animal, what is to be gained if you become an animal too? Two animals do not make for harmony nor do two wrongs make a right. Jesus said, "Love your enemies . . . that you may be sons of your Father" (Mt. 5:44-45). Which is to say: Stop resisting and start loving. Get yourself back in the flow.

It is a difficult lesson, but an important one, to admit that your sudden flare-up of anger evidenced that beneath the facade of composure, there was chaos within you on that morning. Thus you were disturbed by what happened because you were *disturbable*. If you had been in a more loving consciousness, you probably would have dealt with the whole thing in an entirely different way. You might have said to yourself, "I guess she was as intent on getting that seat as I was, and she might not even have seen me. Perhaps now she feels as badly about what happened as I do."

An even more difficult self-admission is that because you were out of the consciousness of the flow, you may well have attracted the experience to you in the first place. This may be the reason why "everywhere I go I run into this kind of behavior." It is consciousness outforming itself. As Shakespeare says, "The world is full of griefs and graves, who knows but that the darkness is in man?"

It may seem naive and impractical, but actually, if you could realize the importance of keeping consciously in the flow of life and the danger of getting out of this flow even for one instant, you might see the whole episode on the subway in the light of what is revealed about you. If you really knew that your behavior in the face of your struggle for the seat indicated a red light warning of a crisis of consciousness, you might have bowed low before the woman and said (perhaps not literally but at least figuratively within yourself), "Thank you, for you have been instrumental in revealing to me that I am out of the flow." And then, grateful for the reminder, you should have taken a quiet moment to "be still and know . . . I am in the flow."

Who but a St. Francis or a Gautama Buddha or a Jesus could act in such a manner? Certainly, it would not be easy. But then what overcoming in life is easy? This kind of creative nonresistance may well be the only practical way to deal with such things. Any other reaction will simply perpetuate the kind of consciousness that enabled it all to happen in the first place, and that will most certainly lead to other such happenings with possibly much more serious consequences.

When Jesus said, in effect, "Pray for those who despitefully use you," He indicated the need to elevate your thoughts about them, for they are *your* thoughts that are obstructing the flow in *your* mind. You may feel that you have thought about the other one enough already. You haven't really thought about *her* at all. You have simply mulled over your erroneous concept of her. You may say, "Oh, people are all alike." But *persons* are not all alike. They are unique and individual, and with personal problems and conflicts that come when they get out of the flow. The Truth is, if you could really know this person and she could really know you, there would be only love between you. For that is the reality of life which human experiences and one's reactions to them tend to obscure.

One man was beside himself over a co-worker. For years he had resented the attitude and behavior of this person, his irritability, his curt manner, and his cold aloofness. Then one day the story was revealed. The irritable one was a widower who had the full care of four young children. He was playing both mother and father to them and thus was preoccupied all the time with the problems of his confused home life. He came to work tired and irritable and personally ashamed that he was doing what appeared to him to be "woman's work" at home. He felt that he was not masculine and that his co-workers were rejecting him. Realizing how wrong he had been, the associate befriended the man. He and his wife "adopted" this family and did many little things to help them to meet their crisis. In time he developed a great fondness for this man, and they became the best of friends.

This reveals a very common human tendency. We tend unrealistically to expect the world to provide us with the kind of peace and security and love which can only come from within ourselves. We do not take people as they are but rather as fits or misfits of our standards and expectations. Then we either reject them outright or we try to change them or make them over to suit our concept of what they should be. This gives rise to the erroneous idea of making friends. Normally a friend is one who agrees with you or one who you have converted to your way, and the friendship lasts as long as he or she remains converted. In Truth, you cannot make a friend, you can only *accept* a friend.

And this acceptance involves a form of *namaskar,* the Sanskrit word that means "I salute the divinity within you."

In Greek mythology, there is a character named Procrustes, who was something less than the perfect host. Overnight guests were always invited to sleep in the "Procrustean bed." In a perverted sense of hospitality, he insisted that they fit the bed perfectly. If they were too short for the bed, he would stretch them to fit. And if they were too long, he would simply cut off their legs. This is the origin of the term *procrusteanism.* It means the tendency to insist that everyone conform to your concept of how they should be.

No matter who the person may be, accept him or her as a person. The person may not be like you and may not like you. Let him or her be! You may not agree with the standards by which the person lives and works. But they are not necessarily wrong because they are different. Be willing to grant that he or she is in the flow of the creative process within. By so doing, you will stay in the awareness of the flow expressing in you and as you.

In the urban situation in which most of us live and work, we are forever being thrown into relationships with persons with whom we have little in common. We are attracted to some persons and others are drawn to us. This is the outforming process of consciousness. However, in our world, few persons are able to determine who they are to work with. People are assigned to jobs by skills and experience rather than by temperament. This may not be the best way, but it is the way it is done. Thus people may well find themselves spending half their waking hours working closely with someone whom they might otherwise find unattractive, disinteresting, or downright difficult. What can they do?

Work, like every important area of life's experience, is a fine opportunity to grow. There is talk of "soft jobs," or of "interesting work," but this is an unrealistic approach to life. In this same consciousness, it may be asked, "What does the job pay?" This reflects the expectation that life and the means of living it come from without. Actually, life flows from within. In the largest sense, a job doesn't pay. It is in evidence that someone has a need and hires another to fill it. The worker gets into the flow of creativity and as he or she gives, he or she receives. The paycheck does come as a reimbursement, but it is only a symbol of an economic cycle that begins in the flow within the worker. Resistant attitudes frustrate the flow and lead to a curtailment of industry and creativity.

There is no "soft job" except where the worker so makes peace with work and so releases the free flow of creativity that the work seems to do itself. There is no interesting work except where an interested person invests interest and enthusiasm in the tasks at hand. In all cases, it is not the work but the attitude of the worker that makes the difference.

Life is lived from within-out. If you look for security or harmony or cooperation on the outside, you become quickly irritated with co-workers who do not cooperate, with employers who are too demanding, and with employees who are careless and indifferent. What can be done? Get into the flow. Whatever the conditions may be or the caliber or character of the people with whom you must work, the important thing is *you are there*. It is good to affirm: *Wherever I am, there let me be.* This means: Be a channel for the flow of the infinite creative process. If you get and stay in the flow, you will not let the attitudes and antics of other persons squeeze you into their mold; you will let the Spirit within you sustain you with all that you need of love and understanding and of the ideas and creativity to do your work well and to be a bigger person in the process.

What can you do when you are surrounded by people with whom you have little in common, people who may appear to be beneath you, people who even resist your efforts to get along with them? You can turn on more light. "It is better to bring a light than to curse the darkness." You may wonder why you are there. The important thing is that, at the moment, you *are* there. And wherever you are, God is. Wherever you are, there is a flow of light and love.

Take time every morning to get into the flow of love and then to actively project this light and love to all your co-workers. As you salute the divinity in each one and know that no matter how the individual may be frustrating it, the person is rooted in a flow of divine love, suddenly you will know why you are there. You are the light of the world—this particular corner of the world. This is your work. And as you do it well, there will be a rich return in ways material and nonmaterial. Because you are in the flow, you will either experience advancement within the job or, through some new opportunity, advancement from the job.

A person in a dark room may be bumping into obstacles everywhere as he or she fumbles for the light switch. Suddenly he or she touches the switch and the room is flooded with light. Nothing in the room is altered. Nothing is made, added, or taken away. Yet in a flash it is all changed. Whereas it had been filled with menacing objects and hazardous footing, now it has become a place of comfort and utility. In the same sense, we may be embroiled in a horrendous experience with hostile people. If we can turn on the light or get into the flow of transcendent love, a miracle of harmony and understanding may unfold. It has been said, "It takes two to make a quarrel." But what is not often realized is that it only takes one to commence the dissolution process.

Philippe Vernier, a religious mystic who was

martyred under the Nazis in World War II, came through unspeakable treatment with an unshakable faith and a radiant consciousness. The philosophy that he evolved while in his "furnace of affliction" has been a light to countless persons who walked in darkness. He insisted that humankind is a torchbearer of the light of God, that we should not spend our time groaning over what the world lacks but bring it what it needs. He called for all persons to "flame up and shine; lift high the fire of God."

This is what Jesus had in mind as He said, in effect, "Don't be the clogged lantern that chokes and smothers the light, the lamp hidden under a bushel. Let your light shine." Know that you are in the flow of love. Your attitudes will change; people will seem to change. At least they will deal with you in a different way, because you are different. In an unbelievably rapid way, certain persons will be drawn to you, and others will move away from you. As in the turning on of the light, out of chaos will come order and right adjustment.

You may harbor feelings of injustice and the urge to get out from under the burdens of life that you are convinced have been "laid on" you by people or conditions "out there." You may feel that you would have no difficulty in getting along with people if you could get into an environment more conducive to friendship and love. However, the answer is not in finding the right person but in being the right person.

So when you discover that you have a conflict with someone, such as the struggle for the subway seat, it is important to keep your spiritual objectivity. The experience could only have come about because you were out of the flow. Thus the way to "get along" in this instance is to "go along" with the full process of what is taking place. The fight for the subway seat reflects an obstruction in the flow of love and harmony. If you resist it and harbor resentment toward it, you assure the recurrence of similar situations in the future. If you get into the flow of understanding and forgiveness, you will dissolve the obstruction and "go along" in life's unfolding process.

Don't delude yourself, this is not easy, because the *ego* is very much involved. "She has no right; that seat is mine." These errant thoughts must be dealt with. There is a self of you that is above such attitudes and which must assert its mastery. You can affirm: *No one can take my good from me. It is more important to have my inner peace than to fight over a seat. It is better to stand in strength than to sit in weakness, to stand in love than to sit in bitterness, resentment, or hatred.*

When you have resolved your own ego-blocked flow of love, releasing a radiant stream of forgiveness and compassion, you can look upon the other person with a view that says, "I know that you are not really aware of what you have done to me or even what you are doing to yourself. I bless you and see you in a flow of love that may provide a whole new kind of environment where you can relax your hostility and unblock your own frustrated flow of love."

And then . . . you can and should let it all go. Above all, "See thou tell no man!" Don't go through the day telling everyone who will listen how this woman in the subway knocked you down to get a seat. Let it go. The more you talk about the experience, the more apparent it becomes that the problem is not the other person, but you.

In the lore of Eastern religions, there is a story of two Buddhist monks journeying on foot through the countryside. They encountered a woman in fear of crossing a rain-swollen stream. Both monks were aware of their sacred vow never to touch a woman. However, one of them was moved with compassion. So he lifted her to his shoulders and carried her to the other side. The monks continued their journey, but mile after mile, the second monk nagged at the first one for breaking his vow. Finally, the first one said, "My brother, I simply carried the damsel across the stream, but you have been carrying her for the last half hour."

To get along with people, one must be willing to *go along* in the flow of life. How many persons become needlessly burdened by the behavior of members of their family, the idlers in their community, and the crime or lack of integrity of the notorious figures that cross the TV screen every day. These burdens are dangerous because they lead to stress and all sorts of emotional disorders. There is scientific evidence today to indicate that this process gives rise to bodily ills all the way from fatigue, to ulcers, to heart trouble, to cancer.

Should you then be indifferent to people or circumstances? Not at all. It is your world. Certainly, do what you can do. But if there is nothing constructive that you can do, then it is folly to engage in self-destructive bitterness or anger or worry or fear. To get along in the world or with the world, you must stay in the flow of life. Sometimes the best way to get along with people is to get along without them. Let go . . . and walk on.

A woman was commiserating on all the problems of her life. A friend, trying to console her, said, "But my dear, you are tearing yourself apart by your anguish. Why not let it all go and find a sense of inner peace." The unrelenting woman replied, "Oh, I just couldn't do that. I think when the Lord sends me tribulations, it is my duty to tribulate." She was wrong on two counts. The Lord doesn't send tribulations. Difficulties in life or in any kind of human relationships come purely and simply because we get out of the consciousness of the flow of love and harmony. And secondly, our responsibility, as the word implies, is our response to God's ability. We have been responding to things "out there." Now we must "let God remold our minds from within." Respond to the ceaseless flow of life. Then you can stand steadfast in the face of the "slings and arrows of outrageous fortune" and affirm: *None of these things move me.*

Every morning, before setting out into the world, or before making the initial contact with the world through watching or reading the morning news, it is the better part of wisdom to prepare yourself by a prayer or meditation to get consciously in the flow of life. It is a simple matter of getting your lights turned on before you face any darkness in the world or in human behavior. In the flow of love, you will tend to see and respond to the divinity in all persons. Instead of expecting the world and the people in it to make your day happy or harmonious, you will establish yourself in the kind of consciousness that you desire to experience, letting it flow forth through you and go forth from you.

Remember, life is lived from within-out. As long as you think that your security or happiness depends on what people do to you or around you, you will anxiously watch that no one threatens your position or tampers with your rights, and you will be ready to do battle with those who do. The symbol of this consciousness is the closed fist, evidencing tension, frustration, and hostility.

Try an experiment for a moment. Hold out your hands. Clench your fists tightly. This is a two-fisted symbol of frustration and force. Can't you feel your whole being reflecting a defensiveness, even a readiness to fight? If you should go forth in this consciousness, the chances are good that you would need to fight. When the fists are clenched, the mind is tense, and thoughts of anger, defensiveness, and fear surge into your consciousness. Approach people with fists clenched and watch them clench their own.

Now open your hands and let them fall to your side or comfortably in your lap. Watch your tensions leave and your whole body relax. Notice how your whole mentality seems to open up and your resistance dissolve. The open hand can hold no weapon. It is a symbol of goodwill and peace. The open hand can pat someone on the back, lift someone up, grasp hands in a common cause . . . and type a letter, paint a picture, plant a garden, and turn the pages of a book.

Closed hands hold on possessively to both people and situations—open hands let them go. Open hands symbolize a readiness to accept the flow. Hold your hands out in a posture of readiness: palms up, hands together, forming a cup or receptacle. Some persons prefer always to pray or meditate in this posture. Don't make a fetish out of such a thing, but it can be helpful if you see it as a symbolic gesture of readiness to receive the fullness of the flow of life.

Now take a few moments in quiet reflection. Sit comfortably in your chair, with your hands held loosely in your lap—for this time with palms up and hands cupped together. Then let something like this thought move easily through your consciousness as an affirmative prayer:

Here I am, Father, use me as an instrument of Your love . . . an agency of Your peace. I am in the flow of life, and I relate easily and lovingly, patiently and understandingly with all persons. I know that no matter what any person is or does, what I am and what I do can most certainly enable me to get along. It may mean that I will get along easily with the person, or it may mean that I will let him or her go and get along without the person. But in every case, I know that my responsibility is simply to keep in the flow, to keep seeing with eyes of love, to be willing to receive and to be responsive to the all-sufficient flow of life, love, and wisdom. I go forth in the joyous certainty that whatever person or situation may come to me in this day, it will be good, for I will be in the flow of good. And if I should have even a fleeting moment of concern, I will simply let go ... and let flow.

CHAPTER 6

The Wellspring
of
Giving

During the Christmas season every year people are caught up in the holiday spirit, giving rise to a frantic giving of gifts and exchanging of greeting cards. It is an interesting study of human nature and of contemporary values. It is quite normal for the giving to be materialistic, status-laden, conformity-ridden, and exhausting. In a sense, much of the giving is actually defensive: "They sent us a card so we must send one right back." "He gave me a ten-dollar scarf, so I must give him something for at least ten dollars." It is like saying, "I can't let them put me under obligation."

Every year there is a cry to put Christ back into Christmas! But it is doubtful if anyone really knows what that means. The greater need is for a new insight into the flow of life and the realization that true giving is *giving way* to the flow.

Jesus, in one of His Beatitudes, gives an important key to the effective life: "Blessed are the meek, for they shall inherit the earth" (Mt. 5:5). It doesn't appear to be a realistic rule for living in modern times. If He had said, "they shall inherit heaven," it might be more acceptable. But "they shall inherit the earth!" Certainly it would appear that it is the strong and aggressive, not the meek, who win the plums of life, who take over the earth.

The Greek word *praeis*, translated as "meek," actually means "tame." It is the opposite of wild and unrestrained. It refers to the person in harness, in control of oneself, one who is established at the center of one's spiritual gravity, one whose consciousness is in focus, who is in the flow of life.

There is an oriental saying, "Meekness compels God Himself." God is the dynamic flowing process of the universe, that which flows in and through man from within-out. Thus Jesus is saying, "Blessed are the meek for they *give way* to the flow of the eternal givingness of God." This is an exciting new insight. True giving is not something you do to or for someone, but it is your consent to let the flow of God flow through you to that someone. Whereas the emphasis is usually on what you give to, the most important thing is what you give *from*.

The word *giving* has been so completely identified with pious acts of philanthropy that it is difficult to think of the word without relating it to the commercial of the church. The emphasis has been on what the gift is to and what rewards come back in the form of "heavenly grace," priestly blessings, a name on the stained-glass window, and a healthy deduction on the tax return.

Churches have failed to teach the truth about giving, primarily because they have been concerned with their own need to receive. Now certainly an effective church is worthy of the support of its congregation, but fundamental to that effectiveness is helping people to understand the principle of giving. It is not enough to prod people to give to something, for it can become routine and perfunctory. People need to know what they give *from*, and thus to consciously *give way* to the divine process.

Here is a riddle to ponder: A cup comes to the faucet for water. The faucet opens and lets the water flow forth to fill the cup. Has the faucet given to the cup? Or has the faucet been involved in receiving from its source, with the cup simply cooperating in the process? Is the cup simply receiving water? Or is it actually giving by being receptive to a process wherein the faucet may receive more? It is not important to determine a right answer—only to keep asking the question. It might be used as something to ponder in meditation, like a *koan* to a Zen Buddhist.

There is so much more to giving than philanthropy, charitable service, and tithing to a church. These are commendable and important. However, there is a possibility that the giving may be "to be seen of men," for ego fulfillment and personal recognition. Jesus said that such persons already have their reward. They wanted human recognition and they received it. However, the true giving process, entailing a flow from within-out, may not have been fulfilled at all.

Kahlil Gibran, in his classic work *The Prophet*, sets the highest tone on giving:

> You give but little when you give of your possessions.
>
> It is when you give of yourself that you truly give....
>
> There are those who give little of the much which they have—and they give it for recognition and their hidden desire makes their gifts unwholesome....
>
> And there are those who give with pain, and that pain is their baptism.
>
> And there are those who give and know not pain in giving, nor do they seek joy, nor give with mindfulness of virtue;
>
> They give as in yonder valley the myrtle breathes its fragrance into space.
>
> Through the hands of such as these God speaks, and from behind their eyes He smiles upon the earth.

This suggests two distinct kinds of giving: (1) Giving that is *outer-centered* which depletes the giver, and (2) giving that is *inner-centered* which endows the gift with that which transcends its intrinsic value; and which so blesses the giver that, like the faucet filling the cup, he or she is immediately and correspondingly filled from within.

If you see a need, and out of a sense of duty or sympathy, give to that need, your giving is outer-centered. On the other hand, if, when you see a need, you turn to the realization of the all-sufficiency of God, and then give not just to the need but *from* the consciousness of divine supply, then your giving is inner-centered. It is a subtle distinction, but knowing this process and acting upon it are the most important insights to effective living.

When the giving is outer-centered, it is a personal thing, and the ego is very much involved. There is a need to be seen and appreciated, and if there is none, the giver is likely to feel hurt or to cry, "Such ingratitude!" But when the giving is inner-centered, it is impersonal. The emphasis is not on the gift itself or to whom or what it is given, but on the inner source of love and substance from *which* it is given. The act of giving is a *giving way* to the flow that springs forth from the wellspring of all-sufficiency. And there is no sense of depletion in the giving, for the giving is also a receiving. Because the act is finished in the giving, there is no expectancy of reward or appreciation. In the *inner chamber*, which may be Jesus' term for "in the flow," the "Father who sees in secret will reward you" (Mt. 6:6).

Outer-centered giving is most often withheld because of a sense of personal inadequacy, postponed to that nebulous future when things will be different: "When I get that raise in salary or the commissions from the deal I am going to make, then I am going to tithe and do so much for my church and for my pet charity." Inner-centered giving is a spontaneous flow that uses any and all means as channels. It is giving of what is available now, but the gift is maximized by the love and praise and gratitude that flow forth from within.

This is made clear in that instance where Peter and John were accosted by a beggar at the gate of the temple (Acts 3:1-9). The poor man had been crippled all his life. It is not being judgmental to say that he was out of the flow. One who begs from life, either through his attitudes toward his employers or from society in general, is out of the flow of his own wellspring of inner support. Remember, Jesus said, " It is your Father's good pleasure to give you the kingdom." One who is asleep to the realization of his true being stands at the crossroads of life with his begging bowl in hand.

It is obvious in this account that the disciples were in a high state of consciousness. They were truly in the flow. For if their first thought had been of sympathy for the "poor beggar," they would have supported his lack by putting some morsel into his begging bowl. And though they might have felt pious for helping an unfortunate creature, they would have gotten out of the flow by doing so.

However, Peter maintained a cosmic perspective. Instead of emphasizing the need of giving to the man's lack, he turned his thoughts inward and gave *from* the source of inexhaustible substance. He said to the man, "I have no silver and gold, but I give you what I have; in the name of Jesus Christ of Nazareth, walk" (Acts 3:6). And the man was instantly and completely healed. The man was crying out for charity, but his real need was to get back into the flow of life, to become a self-reliant person. An outer-centered gift would have supported him in his life as a beggar. The inner-centered gift opened the way for a new life of freedom.

If we consider the story in the context of modern behavior, the reaction to the "beggars" of life might be, "I have much silver and gold, here is my very important gift. You should be very grateful," or, "I have little silver and gold. I am having a hard time myself, so, I am sorry, but I can't help you." In both cases there is a lack of understanding of the true principle of giving.

The actual treatment of beggars is not the subject of this discussion. Certainly it is a problem in our time in which dollar solutions have proved to be totally inadequate. Not that we should be unsympathetic toward the underprivileged persons around us, but we should realize how important it is, for their sake and ours, to understand the process of inner-centered giving. It takes bigness of heart to let go the ego, to truly give way so that the transforming power of God may flow forth. The "flow" may be in the form of bread in the begging bowl, but it may also be in the form of food for the soul that will be directed toward inner changes that are real and lasting. Of course, the unfortunate persons will need, also, to give way. They must be willing to entertain the idea that they are more than beggars, and that if they get in the flow of the creative process, miracles of change can be wrought in and through them.

There is a wellspring of infinite life, substance, and intelligence within you, and yours is the privilege, at any time, of giving way to its flow. Whether it is in your own life or in the life of another, if there is lack of any kind, the Truth is: Something is blocking the flow. The most effective remedy: Give! There is an old axiom, "When things get tight, something's got to give." This does not mean something over which you have no control; it means you. You must give—by giving way to the flow.

A pioneer teacher of this "new insight of Truth" had an interesting approach in counseling. People of all levels of life and in all kinds of personal need came to her for treatment. No matter what else she did for them, she always insisted that, before they left the room, they must make a commitment to some kind of giving. She would stress the Truth that if they wanted help or healing, they had to open the channel by giving way. This giving could be a "thanks offering" for her prayer help (though there was no suggestion to do so). But it could be the idea of doing something for another person or giving away some seldom-used possession. Her favorite text was, "As you give so shall you receive." The emphasis was always on that word *as*. To this teacher, it was a matter of inexorable principle in which there were no ifs, ands, or buts. As you give, in the very move to give, you open the way to the inner flow. She always said, "Your giving *is* your receiving."

We are forever in the presence of an infinite and eternal energy from which all things proceed. Thus it is never for lack of life, substance, intelligence, or love that we experience difficulties but because we are out of the flow. And one of the most effective ways of getting back into the flow is through giving. We may have been thinking lack, thinking "get" or the need to "get." Now we must "think give"!

The giving principle and process pertain to every aspect of life. For instance, everyone harbors in his or her heart a secret desire to be a success in life, but not everyone has discovered the wonder of giving. How often people look for opportunities that might lead to success, and yet shun and even resist demands made upon them that do not seem related to that quest. They might even say, "What's in it for me?" When we understand the full implications of the flow of life, it might be more propitious to say (or feel), "What's in me for the world?" Jesus says the kingdom is within us. Are we ready to give way to its flow?

Many years ago a man and his wife, unable to find lodging for the night, came to a small Philadelphia hotel. The manager gave them his own room because all other rooms were filled. It was no gesture prompted by some self-interest. He didn't know the people, and no one might ever know about his act. He was simply one of a breed of managers who believed that service was the most important product of any business enterprise. Actually, the travelers were Mr. and Mrs. William Waldorf Astor. Some years later when the Waldorf-Astoria Hotel was built in New York City, Mr. Astor would insist on having as its manager the manager of that obscure Philadelphia hotel. Thus did George C. Boldt become the greatest hotel man of the times. When you are in the flow, as he most certainly was, then "all things work together for your good."

When the faucet gives water to the cup, it actually creates a need for a replenishing flow. In physics, this need would be called a *vacuum*. Because nature abhors a vacuum, the need draws the supply. Paul refers to this when he says, "And my God will supply every need of yours according to his riches " (Phil. 4:19). Wanting something is not enough. The desire must lead to giving in some way, which is a giving way to the greater flow.

This is a principle that can be observed everywhere in nature: The polar bear has a white coat of fur because he needs it for camouflage. A duck has webbed feet because he needs them. The ditch digger develops bulging muscles because he needs them. A flabby clerk has no muscles because he doesn't need them. He may wish he had them, but no strength will come until he creates a legitimate need by using more of what he has. Exercise will not make him strong. Actually it tears down the muscle cells. But exercise will establish a legitimate need for strength. And once the need has been established, the strength flows into the muscles as a matter of course. It is a universal process with great bearing on the matter of giving and living.

There may be times when you cannot find the help you need, but there is never a time when you cannot give way to the inner flow and be a source of help for someone else. And it is in giving that you establish your legitimate need and thus open the way to receive. Harry Emerson Fosdick used to say that when you are earnestly set on being useful, you are in a country where you can dig anywhere and strike water.

There is a lot of talk about "positive thinking." Normally it is considered purely in an outer-centered context, thinking positively to make things happen "out there." In a sense, there is no such thing as "positive" and "negative" thinking—only the use we choose to make of the creative power of thought. Thought is always creative. The power we use to make ourselves sick is the same power we use to make ourselves well. The dynamics of the universe flow in a positive stream. So, when we speak or think negatively, we frustrate the flow of this stream. The choice to think positively sustains us within the stream; it is the will to "give way" to the inner flow.

Much "positive thinking" is tense and willful for it is centered in the ego, motivated by the acquisitive instinct. In other words, it is thinking *get!* The need is to think *give!* to give way to the inner flow. We become so involved in "willing" that we forsake the power of "letting." Jesus said, "Your Father knows what you need before you ask him" (Mt. 6:8). Couple this with His promise that it is the Father's good pleasure to give you the kingdom, and we realize that the answer is always within.

To think positively is to synchronize thought with the flow of life. Then, as with the process of the faucet flowing forth to the cup, when the thought is in the flow, it becomes the very mind-energy that flows forth to sustain it. This is the consciousness Jesus implied when He said, " The word which you hear is not mine but the Father's who sent me" (Jn. 14:24). Positive thinking should not be an attempt to make something happen by the power of our ego-directed words. Rather, it should be the will to think God's thoughts after Him, and to "let" His kingdom come, His will be done, in Earth as it is in heaven.

When we think *give!* not only will our thought be in the flow of spiritual power, which will invest our own words with creative power, but also, we will become ready and willing channels for giving in life's relationships, which in turn will draw even greater good to us. It is a continuing cycle that is always in evidence with the healthy-minded person.

A man was extremely despondent over his life. He had been laid off from an important position with a large corporation. It was a typical case of "too young to retire and too old to get work." He was sitting on a park bench, brooding over his situation which appeared quite hopeless. He became aware of the sound of crying. He ignored it at first, for he had his own problems to cry over. As the sobbing continued, he looked around and discovered it was a young girl. At first, annoyed at this disturbance of his gloom session, he was thinking, Why won't she stop? Finally, following his humane instincts, he went over to the girl and tried to comfort her. In time he gained her confidence, and she related her story. She was unemployed and alone in the city. She was too proud to return home and admit that she had failed in her career attempt. Her situation had become desperate, and she was actually contemplating suicide. The man, forgetting himself, talked to the girl as if she were his own daughter. He encouraged her, helped her to find a new attitude. And he suggested some contacts that she might make. Soon the girl went off smiling and with new hope shining in her eyes.

The man sat incredulously trying to assess what had happened, for now, for some strange reason, his own hope had been restored. In this short exchange with the young girl, his own life had taken on new meaning. He realized that, while he had been brooding over his needs, he was further frustrating the flow of his good. When he began to think *give*, there was a letting go, a giving way. He actually forgot himself in his compassion for this forlorn creature. The frustrated flow was unblocked, his perspective returned, and "in the twinkling of an eye," he was in the flow and life was good again.

That very night the man received a phone call, inviting him to start work on an important project that meant a whole new beginning in his life. And, as if to demonstrate the flow in a tangible way, the next afternoon he received a totally unexpected check in the mail. A bad debt that he had long since written off was being repaid. All of this—just because he "gave way" to the flow.

Great energy and creativity are pent up within every person. It is rare, if ever, that one person lives up to his or her potential. As the poet says, most persons die with all their music in them. This is why, in a time of great stress or emergency, one may suddenly release a power unknown to him or her before. Without the pressures of outer-

centered involvement in life, free from the domi-
nance of the ego, the person turns from fretting to
letting, from will to willingness, from getting to
giving. Suddenly he or she is in the flow of unbe-
lievable power.

Time magazine, a few years ago, reported the
story of an invalid woman in a rural area in Florida.
Recuperating from a lengthy illness, she was sitting
in her wheelchair on the front porch of the family
home. Her son was in the front yard, under his
automobile, which he had removed the wheels
from and placed on blocks. Suddenly there was a
lurch, and the car fell on top of the boy, threaten-
ing to crush the life out of him. At the woman's cry,
the husband came running, tried desperately to lift
or pry the car off his son, but to no avail. So he
jumped in his car and sped off to find help. As the
groans grew fainter, the mother knew she must
help. But how? She hadn't walked in months. In a
flash she realized it was life or death for her son,
and she was the only one to help. She raised
herself shakily to her feet and walked unsteadily to
the car. Bracing herself, she lifted. The car raised
a few inches, just enough to let the boy scramble
free. Then she collapsed to the ground. The doctor
was called. Other than some strained muscles, she
was unharmed. Incredulous over the fact that what
appeared to have happened did actually happen,
the doctor said, "I will always wonder how far she
might have lifted that car if she had been well and

strong!"

How could such a thing happen? It is not enough to say, "It was a miracle!" Such a conclusion denies the creative flow of life and our relationship to it. This woman had always been a radiant center of God-life, as all persons are. But, like most persons, she lived in a consciousness far below her optimum. Now, through a sincere desire to give, she actually gave way, let go of her preconceived notions about herself and let the energy of the universe flow into and through her.

A frail invalid lifted an automobile! Startling as such occurrences may be, we need to see them as an evidence of the supportive process of the universe that is always present in every person as a Presence. No matter how great or how desperate the need, within every person is a wellspring of life which is readily available—if we can just give way.

Life is a flowing experience, and within every person is an inlet that may become an outlet to all there is in God. And there is a divine desire to flow forth as life, substance, love, and intelligence. All that is required is that we give way, let it be, let God be God in us. Think *give!* for life is lived from within-out.

St. Francis of Assisi, in effect, said it this way:

> Grant that I may not so much seek to be
> consoled as to console;
> To be understood as to understand;

To be loved as to love . . .
For it is in giving that we receive.

CHAPTER 7

Life Comes
to
Pass

Out of the legendary past comes the story of an Eastern monarch, plagued by worries and harassed at every turn, who called his counselors and wise men together. He asked them to formulate a motto, a few magic words that would help him in times of trial or distress. It must be brief enough to be engraved on a ring so that he could have it always before his eyes. It must be appropriate for every situation, as useful in prosperity as in adversity. It must be a motto wise and true and endlessly enduring, words by which a person could be guided all his life.

The counselors and wise men went off and debated and reasoned and prayed. Finally, they came back to the monarch with the magic words: words for every change or chance, words to fit all situations, words to ease the heart and mind in all circumstances. The words that were engraved on the ring were: *This, too, shall pass away.*

Life is a flowing experience, and the only certainty is change. In fear and in greed, in joy and in sadness, there is a human tendency to hold on. When life is equated with things or with relationships or with moments of fulfillment, the threat of their loss or change is too much to endure. Thus the discovery of the flow of life is the greatest awakening of consciousness we can achieve.

A little girl had a great fear of tunnels. Whenever she was riding on a train or in an automobile with her parents, she would hide her face and bury her head in her mother's lap the moment they entered a tunnel. As the years passed, she discovered that tunnels were not as fearsome as she had believed. Eventually she remarked that she liked tunnels because "they have light at both ends." This is a very significant thing to remember. In going through the dark tunnels of life, there is light at both ends!

The Psalmist sings: "Even though I walk through the valley of the shadow of death, I fear no evil" (Ps. 23:4). We need to give special emphasis to that word *through*. There are times when we seem to be dwelling in the valley. But the Psalmist says, "Though I walk through the valley . . . I fear no evil." He knows that the valley is open at both ends, that life is a flowing experience, and that the dark shadows of the valley will eventually give way to the light of a new day and a new experience.

We often think of death as the supreme reality, or at least the one great certainty. But death is only a tunnel through which we pass from sunlight to sunlight. Grief over death, too, is a tunnel, with light at both ends—something we pass through. It is the most difficult of experiences. But we must know that "this, too, shall pass," and let the divine law of adjustment lead us through the valley into new light and understanding. Life goes on, and we can find new opportunities for love and happiness if we move with it. The "flow of life" is an extremely important concept in relationship to death and all things pertaining to it. We will later devote an entire chapter to the discussion.

The thing that makes the difference in people and in the various circumstances they face is that some persons let the tunnel experience become a static thing, bemoaning that "there is no justice," that "this is the end; my life is over." Others, however, keep on keeping on, and they find growth and betterment as a result of each experience.

Physical handicaps have made cowards and weaklings of many persons. Great heartaches and misfortunes have caused many to give up, to make their beds in the valley of misfortune and ultimately to become bogged down in self-pity, bitterness, and disillusionment. But there are others, those like Beethoven, Stevenson, Milton, Steinmetz, and Helen Keller who, going through dark tunnels of adversity, have been spurred on to new achievement. The attitude in which the difficulty is met makes all the difference.

If you are faced with a challenge, refuse to be panic-stricken. Life has not ended for you. Life flows on. Declare for yourself: *I accept the reality of this situation, but not its permanence.* Certainly, there is no point in hiding your head in the sand. The experience is there to be met. Determine that you will meet it, but on your terms. Do not let the outer happening squeeze you into its box, but open your mind to the flow of wisdom, love, and good judgment by which you can deal masterfully with it. Stand tall as you affirm: *I meet this circumstance in complete confidence that He who is in me is greater than he who is in the world. I do not deny its reality, but I deny its permanence. I know that this, too, shall pass away.*

Once, when I was facing a disturbing situation that had settled like a weight on my shoulders, I was leafing through the Scriptures haphazardly, and my eyes suddenly focused on the words "it came to pass." This is an oft-repeated phrase in the Bible that has no special meaning in itself. But suddenly the words had a special meaning for me: This challenge did not come to stay. "It came to pass." No matter how real or substantial it seemed to be, it would pass away, just as every other undesirable situation before it had done. It had come to bring me something I needed for my own growth. But now it would pass on into oblivion.

The moment this little glimmer of light came, the burden was instantly lifted from my shoulders. And as I let go of my concern over the problem, it swiftly moved in the direction of an amazing resolution. It was almost as if my anxiety had been preventing the solution—like holding a compass needle and then seeing it float easily back to fix on magnetic north as you let it go.

No matter how real or frightening a situation may be, it is still a transitory thing. Only the good is real and lasting. Look back in your life and recall the times when you were frantic over some crisis, when you were bogged down in some grievous misfortune that seemed to be the end of everything. Where is that challenge now? Where are the people who were standing in the way of your good? Where are those circumstances that seemed to have you hemmed in? Where are those burdens that seemed beyond endurance?

Francois Villon sighs, "Where are the snows of yesterday?" Obviously, yesterday's snows have become part of today's trees, plants, rivers, and oceans. All of them have been transformed completely, transmuted into new life and new forms. At any season of the year, one can get into the consciousness of the universal flow just by meditating on the inexorable movement of nature's processes from the infilling of winter to the outforming of spring, to the richness of summer to the harvest of fall. Nothing stays; all is change; it comes to pass.

Why do children go to school? To be confronted with challenges that will stimulate their growth as people. They certainly don't come to school to fail; they come to pass. If you look back to the early years of your life, you may recall experiences in the third grade or the sixth grade. You may remember the teachers, the associations, some of the experiences. They were all real and vital and important to you at the moment. But all you can say about them now is that "they came to pass."

The experiences of today are simply grade levels in the ongoing process of life. We are not here to fail; we are here to pass. No matter how happy or fulfilling the present experience may be, you can't keep it as it is any more than you can hold back the tides of the sea. Like the "manna from heaven" that the Israelites were blessed with in their wilderness experience, today's good is for today, to be used and then loosed. This is the continuing process of the flow of life.

One man was sentenced to five years in the penitentiary. When the prison doors closed behind him, he was filled with fear, then self-pity, then hostility. He knew he had committed a crime for which he had to pay the penalty. But he couldn't relate himself to the kind of people who were there and to the general atmosphere of the prison. He resented the place; he resented and hated the prisoners, the guards, the warden. He began to feel that the whole world was against him. Some of the prisoners tried to be friendly, but he refused to have anything to do with them. He cursed them and everyone connected with the institution. Needless to say, he was terribly unhappy.

One day he met a trustee who put him wise to himself. This unusual prisoner helped him to see the unexpected possibilities in his prison experience. He was brutally frank: "Look, if you start doing something worthwhile, these five years will pass before you know it. Why not spend your time getting ready for the day when you'll get out of here? You're not hurting anyone but yourself by the attitudes you've been displaying. It's about as silly as banging your head against the cell wall. Why don't you quit fighting and start being friendly toward people? You'll find in time that this isn't such a bad place after all. If you take advantage of the opportunities the years offer, your term here can be as useful to you as a college education."

These words rang through the new prisoner's mind for many days. They began to make sense. So he started changing his attitude. Needless to say, he was soon getting along with the other prisoners. He was given a chance to enroll in a class in radio repairing. He found it so interesting that he could hardly wait to get to class every day. He did so well that when the course was concluded, the warden made arrangements for him to take advanced courses in radio and electronics.

The time passed so quickly that at the end of four years, when he was paroled with time off for good behavior, he was actually reluctant to leave.

He didn't feel that he had completed his education yet. He went out to live a well-adjusted life. During World War II he rendered invaluable service to the government, and today he is a highly regarded specialist in the field of electronics. His experience as a prisoner had "come to pass."

There may be experiences in your life that you have thought of as "serving time." But in every case, it is the attitude that counts, the way in which you view the experience. It is important to hold the thought: No matter what the challenge, it has come to pass, not to stay.

As we have discussed it previously, sickness is not the end of life, and certainly not the will of God. It is not the result of some "intent" of nature. Sickness is simply some limitation of mind or body working itself out. The mental and physical causes of the illness may have been present for a long time. But now it has "come to pass," and thus it is on the way out. Don't give too much thought energy to the particular condition, the cold, head-ache, arthritis, or ulcer. Hold the thought that it is now passing out of your mind and out of your body, being dissipated into the nothingness that it is. Of course, you must consciously let go. Since many illnesses are emotionally induced, there may be some subtle fulfillment in the experience. Thus self-honesty and determination are vital. Someone has said, "When you are sick of being sick, you will get well." This, because you come to a point of willingness to let it go, in the realization that it came to pass, not to stay.

A few years ago, due to what I later discovered was a carburetor malfunction, I experienced an embarrassing stalling of my car in the midst of heavy traffic at the toll station of an important bridge, and right at the rush hour. Horns were honking, tempers were flaring, and my starter was grinding. Finally, it ground to a complete stop, as the battery's power was exhausted. At such a moment one easily forgets his spiritual ideas and runs an emotional gamut of frustration, anger, and self-pity. There I was, stalled in unbelievably heavy traffic. What to do? How was I to get out of this fix?

I recall that into my mind came the seemingly irrelevant thought: Tomorrow night at this time I'll be sitting at home relaxed and happy, and this will all be in the past. I chuckled to myself to think that my sense of humor was still working, even in this emergency. Then the full impact of the thought struck me. It was not just a facetious thought, but a great revelation. For in that flash of insight, I tuned in on the flow of life. It was no intellectual analysis of the problem and how to fix it, but it was an assurance that "this, too, shall pass."

What happened? The answer came so quickly that it seemed a miracle. Certainly a skeptical person would find room for debate and ridicule. What power can a change of attitude have on a faulty carburetor or an exhausted battery? Can anxiety and tension on the part of the driver have an influence on the function of a car? And can faith and prayer affect even inanimate things? There is some valid research that has pointed to a resounding yes to this question. What happened for me at that time I don't really know. I only know that I was led to try the starter again. The motor turned over once, and the car was running. In a moment I was speeding across the bridge on my way home. The next night, sitting comfortably in my living room, I looked back on the whole experience with gratitude that my moment of crisis had truly "come to pass."

When you find yourself in any seemingly hopeless situation, it is wise to shun the tendency to emphasize the darkness of the tunnel rather than the fact that the tunnel has light at both ends. When you dwell on the darkness and futility of a situation, you will soon become bogged down in the slough of despond. Keep in the consciousness of the flow of life: "This, too, shall pass."

Every experience in life comes to pass because life is change. This is true not only of unhappy experiences, tragedies, and difficulties but of the happy experiences too. It is true of all worthwhile achievements. When you accomplish a fine thing, achieve some victory or goal, it is not wise to dwell too long on the success or to go on endlessly trying to derive pleasure from it. It has come to pass. The achievement is a growth experience. It brings you that much closer to the greater unfoldment of your innate potential. The law of life is "grow or go." No matter that after one performance you may have the world at your feet; this, too, shall pass. Tomorrow is another day. It brings new opportunities and new demands. You can build on past success, but you cannot rest on it.

A man was observed wearing a large badge that read, "I attended the Century of Progress." It was twenty years after the Chicago fair, but he was wearing this "medal" as his one claim to importance in life. Many of us have a similar compulsion to wear "medals" in the form of the evidences we keep handy of past accomplishments: press clippings, trophies, pictures on the wall, and so on. Certainly it is interesting to know about what has come to pass. History is an exciting study. But history simply records; it doesn't glorify. The "good days" are not the golden days of your youth or the heyday of your success. They are the opportunities and adventures to be found in tomorrow and tomorrow and tomorrow.

It is good to look back and appreciate the blessings that have come into your life. A little nostalgia has never hurt anyone. The danger is that you may become so fond of riding on the "observation car" that you never see where you are going, but only where you have been.

There are those who might accept the thought, "this, too, shall pass," in the context of discouragement. For it might seem to say that the good things in life are fleeting, and we can only appreciate them in retrospect. However, if we get the thought of the "flow of life," we realize that it means that it is in working toward achievement that we gain life's satisfactions, not in the savoring of the achievement itself.

Great is the delusion that "I will be happy when . . ." There is no true happiness in accomplishment, other than the fleeting moment of exhilaration. Life is change. The sale is made and the commission banked. The book is written, the ball game won. Tomorrow we still have to find the vision to meet a new day. There are other sales to make, other books to write, and other games to play. Happiness comes when one knows that he or she is in the flow of life and of the guidance to live it fully and well.

Great are the challenges faced by the young couple who raise a family. Hard as it may be to accept, the fact is that children come into our lives to pass. They come to grow and go. How natural it is for a mother to say, "Oh, I wish I could keep them as little babies all their lives." Of course, it is an idle and quite negative dream. Life is growth, and life is change. In later years one may wish to keep children as nine-year-olds, the precocious little persons one just can't bear to see develop into "problem teenagers." But all too soon they are sporting outrageous hair, playing wild music, and crowding the evening curfews that are set for them. The next thing one knows they are off to college, and into marriage, and work, and on their own. Mother and father often begin at this time to feel left out of the new families that are established. They feel that something has gone out of their lives. But it has only "gone out" because they have been postponing the happiness and fulfillment that come with every experience. It has come to pass.

It is sad to see the empty lives of parents who have never learned to let go of their children, even after long years of separation. The same tragedy can be seen in the husband or wife separated by death without having learned that an experience or a relationship has a blessing of enrichment for the moment. We must take the blessing but move on with life.

When someone we love passes to a new consciousness or into a new experience or even from this plane of life to another plane, it is a positive thing. There is always a constant movement of good. "This, too, shall pass"—both the heartache and the joy. The only way to find a continuing sense of peace and fulfillment is to be adventuresome, to face every day in the consciousness that "this is a new day, and I will accept its blessings and its challenges; I will enjoy it and find fulfillment in it, even though it, too, will pass."

If you are experiencing a physical challenge, you can take hope and strength in knowing that "this, too, shall pass." But when it does pass away and you come out of your tunnel into the light, one thing cannot be overlooked: You will never be the same again! Resist the temptation to get back to the way things were. Remember that in the way things were, there was a subtle storm brewing within you that finally erupted into your illness. Don't look back. Look forward to new experiences. The desire to "get back to normal" is unrealistic. The tests in the sixth grade may be harder (and they should be), but you do not gain anything by trying to get back to the third grade where the tests were easier. (Actually they only seem easier, because you are now seeing them from a sixth-grade perspective.)

Every day of your life comes to pass. Each day is a continuing experience of growth. As Shakespeare put it, "Come what come may, time and the hour runs through the roughest day."[1] It may have been a miserable day, but it came to pass. It has provided you with the challenge to reach for a higher level of consciousness. The sun sets eventually and brings on the release and quiet peace of night, and tomorrow is another day. There is no need to go back over this challenging day, rehearse its story, feel sorry for yourself over it. It came to pass.

Even if it was the best day you have ever had, give thanks for it, and look forward to continued opportunities for growth. You can't hold on to this great day any more than you can stop the progress of the sun across the sky. You have to begin all over again. This is the great leveler of life, an evidence of a divine grace that is constantly involved in the affairs of man. You can't go back, nor can you hold on to today. Life is lived in a series of progressions, the good leading to the better, and the better leading to the best.

Whenever you throw a log on the fire, the wood (as the acorn and the tree) must go, to bring the heat and light of the fire. There is a beautiful line in the Scriptures: "God requireth that which is past" (Eccles. 3:15 KJV). The wood has to lose its identity in the fire. If today is to be fired with enthusiasm, with the light and heat of creative action, the past has to be consumed. We have to let go of the old and face the unfolding "now" of tomorrow and tomorrow, knowing that "this, too, shall pass."

Nothing that happens is final. Isn't that a wonderful Truth? You may look at yourself objectively and say: "Well, I have lived through many challenges, and I've come to know certain limitations that I must allow for. I know myself pretty well after all these years." But what you are really saying is, "What I am is fixed and final, and I might as well make adjustments to it. This is the way I'll always be." But this simply is not true—unless this is the level at which you want to continue to accept life and yourself. This is not the way you really are; it is the way you *think* you are. If you want to remain in the second grade all your life, you can. But you will have a hard time, for eventually you will be bigger than the other children, and even your desk won't fit you.

You may pause at the close of the day, on New Year's Eve, at graduation, or at the time of retirement and look back to view all you have done. Accept what you see as the facts of your experience, but they are not final. You are not "done" yet. You still have within you a dynamic potential for growth, and it *must* come to pass.

Life may seek to label you and type you. A report card or a financial statement may seem to say, "This is what you are." There may be those who will want to measure you by grades and merit badges and achievement certificates. But these say nothing of what you *are* any more than your grades in school reveal what you are. These things usually indicate *where* you are in consciousness and unfoldment. But you are still only part of the way along this great eternal life experience. You came not to live *in* the valley but to walk *through* the valley, and there is light at both ends.

So wherever you are, whatever may have been the challenges of the past, and no matter what you may be facing today, walk on! In the flow of life, there can be no hopeless situation, no incurable illness, no "last straw."

In the final analysis, it is only the intangible

something that we call God that remains unchanged in and through all things. All else is transitory, changing, growing, progressing. All else comes to pass as we continue on the spiraling pathway toward the realization of our own God-potential.

CHAPTER 8

To Grow Old
or
Grow Onward

Joseph McDonald, just past eighty years of age, has been associated in business with a large number of men over the years, but no one had ever referred to him as "Pops" or "Uncle Joe" or "Old Man McDonald." He was one of those unforgettable persons with whom you never associated the idea of age. One day he was lunching with a young associate who was greatly impressed with the octogenarian's vigor, alertness, and apparent youthfulness. The younger man knew that the older one was doing a full day's work in his profession every day and putting many a young man to shame with his achievements. Furthermore, the younger man was impressed by his friend's outlook and his carefully laid plans for the future.

Finally, the young man asked, "Mr. McDonald, if you will forgive the question, how old are you?" The older man turned merry eyes on his questioner, and with a feigned look of reproach, replied, "My son, my age is none of *my* business."

And this is the key to the vigor of his youthfulness. While most men are laying plans for retirement and old age, dreading each coming birthday, and actually making a business of thinking, talking, and acting their age, Joseph McDonald was too busy living and enjoying life to waste time worrying about old age. He would agree with Andre Maurois that growing old is no more than a bad habit which a busy person has no time to form.

We have been conditioned in our culture to think of life as beginning with birth and moving downhill inexorably toward death. The clergy have droned, "From the day we are born we begin to die." This is the "great lie" that we must erase from consciousness. Life does not grow old. Life does not deteriorate. Life does not die. Life is an eternal, dynamic, flowing process.

It is true that for each of us life is consciousness, and we are as old or as young as we think we are. This means that age is basically psychological rather than physiological. "God giveth, and God taketh away," the funeral ritual has said. This has led to rationalistic comments such as, "God hath taken my loved one home." It is this kind of nonsense that has taken the vitality and believability out of religion.

Life is a flowing process, and every person is a specialized channel for that flow. The purpose of life is to live, not to die. While many talk of deterioration and death as God's will, Jesus clearly stated, " It is not the will of my Father ... that one of these little ones should perish." Where is the "home" to which God has taken your loved one? Jesus clearly located the kingdom of heaven as within you not faraway someplace in the skies. Home is the "inner chamber" where you are forever in the flow of life.

Life is not geared for age and deterioration. Actually life is a dramatic process of renewal and regeneration. Medical researchers tell us that there is no physical reason that we must grow old and deteriorate, since the cells are constantly renewed and the body is never older than approximately one year. Thus there is no law of decay and death in God. God, who is life-giving, cannot at the same time be death-dealing.

There is an interesting statement found in the Apocryphal work, the Wisdom of Solomon 1:12-16 NEB:

> "Do not stray from the path of life and so court death; do not draw disaster on yourselves by your own actions. For God did not make death, and takes no pleasure in the destruction of any living thing; he created all things that they might have being. The creative forces of the world make for life; there is no deadly poison in them. Death is not king on earth, for justice is immortal; but godless men by their words and deeds have asked death

for his company. Thinking him their friend,
they have made a pact with him because
they are fit members of his party; and so
they have wasted away."

What are we saying? That one should live forever? No one really knows the potential of the life
span of humankind. There are researchers today
who are suggesting that, in theory at least, human
beings can live forever. But that is not relevant to
this discussion. Length of years is not important.
Quality of life is what counts. Deep from within the
recesses of our being there is that which whispers,
if we could but listen, "I am, I always was, I always
will be."

The important thing is to keep alive as long as
we live. It is a commitment to grow onward rather
than simply to grow old. When asked how she
managed to grow old so gracefully, a retired
midwestern doctor replied, "You don't grow old.
When you stop growing, you *are* old."

Many people begin thinking of age at the time
when they have just acquired the ability to live fully.
They are harassed by the "middle-age syndrome"
with its implications that the rest of life is all
downhill. Middle age is not the beginning of the
end, but the end of the beginning. Anne Morrow
Lindbergh says that it should be a period of shed-
ding shells—the shell of ambition, the shell of
material accumulation and possessions, and the

shell of the ego. It is a time to begin to let go—and walk on.

Contrary to the common human belief, we do not begin to slow down because we are becoming old. We are becoming old because we are slowing down. The cells of our bodies are like water in a river. Motion helps them to stay in the flow and thus to purify themselves. There are literally thousands of moping people who could renew their strength and youthfulness to say nothing of finding freedom from aches and pains, if they would simply stir themselves in mind and body, get into the flow in consciousness and "into the swim" of activities. The wisdom of the world has conditioned us to "act our age." Now we must begin to act our youth—to act our experience in the flow of life.

One of the most obvious ways in which we get out of the flow of life is through our subtle enslavement to the "cult of youthfulness." Actually there is implied a morbid preoccupation with age in the frantic attempt to camouflage it. When we constantly think and talk about ways to appear youthful, we are out of the flow of life. There is nothing wrong with cosmetic aids to youthfulness if they are employed for the purpose of giving us something to live up to and not something to hide behind. Cosmetics cannot give us a renewed spirit.

A well-known plastic surgeon, who has done cosmetic face-lifts on thousands of women, recently expressed his misgivings about such operations. He says that he is saddened to see faces that have had all the lines taken away from eyes that have seen and experienced painful times. He says the face becomes a "lifeless mask" through which the sad eyes peer in contradiction of all that the person seeks to portray in his or her features. The more we reach for the masquerade of youthfulness, the more we get out of the consciousness of the flow, which is the secret of youthfulness.

The most remarkable people we see around us are not the ones who cover their age most effectively but those who are "timeless" in that we do not consider them either young or old. We just enjoy being with them for they have the charm of spiritual liberation. How sad it is to see the frantic efforts of those who create a facade of "youthfulness" behind which they cower in fear that people will discover their age, as if it were some secret crime. Because of the stress involved, their efforts are actually counterproductive. For instance, they may look far more youthful and attractive if they style their hair in their natural gray than if they tint it to a solid black. The important thing is what happens to the spirit of the person, for the strain to appear young evidences a childish inability to see the ongoingness of life.

Life is a continuum, not a discrete series of breaks. Old age should not be another period like infancy, adolescence, or maturity. Ideally it should be a summation of the whole, a flowering experience of fulfillment. It should include and represent the earlier periods, but not obliterate them. There is nothing superior about youthfulness. It is neither a stage to cherish nor to reject. It should be, rather, incorporated within us, along with all the other stages that make up the full spectrum of our total person.

This is obviously what Browning had in mind when he said: "Grow old along with me! The best is yet to be."[1] He is saying, "Grow onward. Don't just settle into the rut of old age." Life is a flow, not a dead-end street. Added years are added opportunities, but you have the responsibility to use them creatively. If you make a full-time job of *trying* to appear youthful, you are actually making a business of age. But age is none of your business! Your true business is "the express business," becoming a creative channel for the flow of life.

At about the time when many persons begin thinking that life is all downhill, Sir Christopher Wren, who built the magnificent St. Paul's Cathedral in London in the seventeenth century, was enthusiastically entering a new career. After serving as professor of astronomy at Oxford University, he turned to architecture. In the forty-one years after his forty-eighth birthday this amazing man executed fifty-three churches and cathedrals, most of which still stand as monuments to his greatness. He was like the man who said he had lived threescore years and ten and had the hang of it now and could do it again!

If you flow with life, every year is a fascinating challenge full of adventure and discovery. If you resist the changes, each year will become a millstone that will gradually bend your shoulders and drag your steps. In the flow of life, there is a constant process of growth. At forty, you should be twice as well-equipped to receive and use the blessings of life as at twenty. At sixty, you should be three times as equipped. At eighty, four times.

It is sad that people permit age to do such awful things to them. In the flow of life, time is not a drag but an opportunity to gain in spiritual stature and beauty of person. Actually, as one gets older in years, one should get cuter and funnier and mellower and more tolerant and more perceptive and wiser . . . and more beautiful in a new and unique way.

A woman reporter traveling in India met an Indian woman of obviously advanced years who had that certain radiant something that made one want to look at her in admiration. The reporter finally said to her, "Madam, you are absolutely beautiful." The older woman replied in deep sincerity, "I ought to be, my dear, for I am over seventy-five." To this woman, the years of her life meant added opportunity to develop true beauty rather than an excuse for deterioration and disfigurement. This is an attitude that every person can and should form.

Instead of decreasing our powers, why should not the continuing years make us even stronger, happier, healthier, and more capable? Why should not the added years provide us with new interest and evoke new ambition in a way compatible with our maturity as the years of our youth did in our teens? Actually, at the time when most of us begin entertaining the terrible falsity about life, we have just acquired our fullest equipment for living. We are just ready to make the best use of our powers. But instead of going forward to full, rich, and expanding lives of usefulness, all too often we methodically set about blocking the flow with signs that boldly proclaim: Too old!

Birthdays are among life's greatest challenges. True, a birthday is a time for happy nostalgia and for a few hours in the center of attention and affection. But birthdays also have strong negative connotations. They tend to set up a crystallized pattern which, because of the emphasis on the point of beginning, makes life a continuous cycle of counting years and anticipating the ending. It is almost as if we erected a tombstone and had it pre-engraved with our name and date of birth, with the date of death to be filled in when that time comes.

In The Book of Job, there is an interesting thought that suggests the concept of "timeless-ness":

"If you will set your heart aright,
   you will stretch out your hands
      toward him....
Surely then you will lift up your face
      without blemish;
   you will be secure, and will not fear....
And your life will be brighter than the
      noonday;
   its darkness will be like the morning.
And you will have confidence, because
      there is hope."
                    —Job 11:13, 15, 17-18

At high noon it is difficult to find your way by the sun, for you cannot tell the direction of its movement, where it rose and where it will set. Thus "life . . . brighter than noonday" would indicate life without the consciousness of length of years, simply the awareness of depth and the intensity of bright, shining enthusiasm, wit, freshness, and vigor. In this consciousness, you will "be like the morning. And you will have confidence, because there is hope."

Many a person who celebrates a birthday has little else to celebrate. As someone has said, "Many people brag about hitting seventy or eighty, who never hit anything else in their life, except perhaps a golf ball or maybe a bottle." It is a cynical statement, but a telling point. Living a certain number of years is nothing to brag about. What matters is how you have lived. But even more important, what are you reaching for now? If you begin to reach today, then this is the birthday of your life.

Much is made of birthdays, but a true birth experience is when you actually give birth to something. In this sense, it is really the mother who gives birth to the child. The date of birth should be her birthday, not the child's. She has justified her existence in the birth process; she has been involved in the greatest creative act. We should really send the cards and gifts to mother on the birthdate. For what did you do at that time that is so important?

If you must have a date to mark as a birthday, why not let it be some time at which you have given birth to something—perhaps the birth of an influential idea, the launching of an important project, or the beginning of a new way of life that has come about because of your own conscious commitment. This is something to be proud of, something for which you can rightly accept from others the blessing of "happy birthday."

Because we have been conditioned to believe that life is to be experienced from the outside, we have set out into the world to get a job, to build a career, to achieve success, and to work relentlessly at trying to reach the "top." Few of us ever set many goals in life beyond those associated with our work or our family. Thus we are swept along on the progressive stages set by promotion scales, retirement ages, and the growth of children, their graduation from school, marriage, and so on. Suddenly we are swept past an invisible boundary into a time where there is little left other than memories and possibly self-reproach for not having achieved more of life's "plums."

Along the way, however, it is possible that one has not really lived his or her own life, or set his or her own goals. They were, more likely than not, corporate goals, family goals. But what of your own secret longings? What do you really want to do with your life? What is most important to you as a person? How would you like to spend the next five years? Not how *will* you or how do you think you should, but how would you like to? Or to see it in another context, how would you live your life if you had just six months to live?

In other words, you need to have goals greater than life, to see your own inner growth and soul expansion as the long-range goals to which you can give increasingly more time, until in "retirement" you can devote full time to it, and with never a feeling of being rejected by life.

One can argue that industry is unwise and unfair in its retirement policies, that creative people are shunted aside and rejected when they have years of potential productivity within them. And it is all true. But the important thing is not what happens to people, but what happens within them. If we are in the flow of life, we will live creatively in work or in retirement. If we are out of the flow, our life will be a study in frustration and boredom, even if we have a steady job. Any time on our own will be spent merely thinking about, recouping from, or resisting the major involvements of our work and family—with no time devoted to self-discovery and the pursuance of individual unfoldment.

When we live in the consciousness that life is to be lived from the outside, our goals tend to be acquisitional rather than personal. Thus if it seems that doors are closing to us in the opportunities to acquire the plums and plaudits from the world, we begin to enclose ourselves in shells. And in the "wisdom of the world which is foolishness with God," we begin to place the emphasis on caution and conservatism and security. We fearfully try to possess life rather than letting it live us, and the more we hold on the more we block the flow.

There are times in one's life—and perhaps this very moment is one of them—when one needs to leave all and walk on. Reject the tendency to settle on a final definition of self. "It is not yet manifest what you should be." Walk on! Don't accept the idea of growing old—simply grow onward.

Retirement, as someone has said, is the greatest shock the system can sustain. But there is no reason for either retirement or the shock. Retirement is a comparatively modern concept, born out of increased efficiencies of automation. There is an increasing trend toward shorter working weeks and earlier retirements. This is fine and good if we know how to keep alive as long as we live. If we remain in the flow of life, we will go forward to live each day as if it were truly the first day of our lives. At an age of ninety-four, Charles Fillmore awakened one morning singing these words: "I fairly sizzle with zeal and enthusiasm, and I spring forth with a mighty faith to do the things that ought to be done by me." And this spirit was reflected in his life, where he was too busy and too excited about growing onward to grow old.

Retirement is all too often thought of as a backing away, getting out from under, taking it easy. We normally plan for retirement as a time when we can go off and do nothing. An exhaustive study made of centenarians turned up the interesting fact that keeping busy was one thing they all had in common. It was found that not one retired-to-do-nothing person had lived to be a hundred. The study concluded that retirement and enforced leisure defeat their own goals and that no one should be put out to pasture, but everyone should go forward to some new kind of challenging activity. Perhaps the word *retirement* has become a stigma. Maybe we should use such words as *advancement, progression,* or *life change*. But whatever we call it, it should be a growing onward and not just an acquiescing in growing old.

Age, in terms of the passing years of your life,

is inevitable; but there is always a choice. You can grow older or you can grow onward. Growing old takes no effort and is usually accompanied by the attitude that life just happens and you can do nothing about it. However, growing onward takes much effort and discipline. One must work at the process of keeping the whole self alive. It may mean being as concerned about what you give your mind for breakfast as what you give your body— giving yourself a steady diet of uplifting, creative, stimulating, challenging, positive ideas.

We now have a whole new class structure in our society, the "senior citizens." But we need to take another look at what we mean by the term and how its negative implications have defrauded millions of persons of their true place in our world. In general, the word *senior* implies achievement, advancement, honor. This is good. But how often the term *senior citizen* tends to mean a useless citizen, one who has been put out to pasture. There are those who are working by political action to change all this. However, it may be that it is an individual matter. The people in the "senior" bracket will need to give emphasis in their own attitudes and self-image to growing onward rather than growing old.

Wherever you may be on the scale of life as measured by years, you are alive as a dynamic channel for the flow of the divine creative process. Society may mandate retirement from a particular job, but no one can force your withdrawal as an integral part of the universe. You should never retire, in the connotation in which the term is normally used. Never get boxed into a position where you are "out of it." The sense of remaining "in" can be acquired in many ways. No matter what your business was, your true business was, is, and always will be the business of releasing the flow of God manifesting in and as you. Perhaps you do not have "gainful employment," but there is much to be gained in doing useful and helpful things. You can mind babies, do odd jobs, attend community meetings, visit sick friends, grow flowers, and pray for the world. And an experienced business person has much to offer in advice and counsel to young business people, particularly those who are disadvantaged or culturally deprived.

A much-beloved minister resigned his post to make a new beginning in a new city. One of his devoted followers, knowing how much he enjoyed reading a locally published syndicated columnist and on finding that it was not published in the town to which he was moving, decided to regularly send them to him. In thirteen years since, he has never missed a monthly mailing from this person, including every column carefully clipped from the paper—over thirty-five hundred individual pieces. He says he often marvels at the commitment of this person, who is now well-advanced in years, thinking that he should not permit her to do this. But then he knows that he would be frustrating the beautifully disciplined effort of this woman to grow onward instead of growing old.

There is a tendency with some people to capitulate to the "rocking-chair syndrome" because of the erroneous belief that age implies a necessary cessation of activity. Time is not toxic. There is no reason that added years should be a poison to the body or the mind. Time is opportunity, and when you have more free time, you have the golden opportunity to continue with education and the kind of growth experiences that so often have been neglected because there was "no time." You can learn to paint, to write, to construct, to perform. Grandma Moses was not simply a genius come to light, but rather an example of how hidden creativity can be released in any person regardless of years, if only the effort is made. Keep challenging yourself with change, new experiences, new faces, and the enchantment of less familiar places.

A matter of great concern to life's "seniors" is the planning of wills and estates and the future disposition of life's accumulations. Great enrichment and fulfillment result from giving, but only from giving now. More people need to seriously consider the axiom: "Give while you live." Many persons are living unhappy, lonely, and meaningless lives, despite the fact that they have provided for much gracious and generous giving after they are gone. Why not receive joy and fulfillment upon making those bequests now, thus getting into the consciousness of the flow of life and substance and giving exciting new meaning to your "senior" years?

Stay in the flow of life no matter what the years may say. If you flow with life, every day will be a fascinating challenge full of adventure and excitement. As the poet says, every day can be a dirge or a life-march as you will. By conscious choice and commitment, march to the music of your own drummer, that inner voice that says keep on—and keep on keeping on! Life is for living! Walter Pitkin says that life begins at forty. Why not sixty? or eighty? Actually, life begins for you every day. This day is the first day of the rest of your life. It is your time to give new birth to the innateness of you. Happy birthday!

And remember, if someone should facetiously inquire as to your age, don't waste your time on the rebuke, "It is none of your business!" Instead, surprise the person and strengthen your own awareness by proclaiming, "My age is none of *my* business. I am, as I have always been, in the flow of life."

CHAPTER 9

Life, Death,
and
Rebirth

Anyone who flows as life flows has solved the enigma of existence. This lovely, lilting thought of Lao-tzu has set the tone of our thesis *In the Flow of Life.* We have dealt with many applications of this concept in human experience, and in summation, it could be said that the idea is both hopeful and helpful. And yet, there is one phase of life that we have not touched on. What about death?

Is life a dead-end street? Is our existence limited to that period between birth and death in which we should "eat, drink, and be merry," for a grim reaper awaits us all in our tomorrow? The concept of the "flow" is an effective means of dealing with the limitations of human experience, but is it rendered inoperative when faced with the void beyond life? What, then, is life?

There are many definitions of life, but most of them are poetic abstractions with little relevance to living. The word *life* is used in many ways, implying widely different meanings. Life is a living organism; it is the unwritten pages of a personal biography. Life is caprice ("That's life for you!"), or life is existence that is terminated by death. However, the reason that the passing of a loved one is such a shattering experience is that our frame of reference is too small. Like living in the flat world of pre-Columbus times, there is a point "out there" where the journeyer on the seas of life simply falls off into oblivion.

How freeing it is to know life as a universal flow! The flow is personalized in you and as you. You are an integral part of the universe, where each part contains within it all the elements of the whole. Thus there is that of you that is more than your physical body, and the *you* that transcends the body is a time-space parenthesis in the universal dimension of eternity. This is what is implied when you affirm: *I am a spiritual being, a whole creature in God.*

The important thing is that you are a unique individualization of God. Whatever else life is, you are in it, you are its livingness, you are here, you are alive and living. But where did you come from? Where will you go when you die? Why are you like you are? And why are other people like they are? Why are people all so different, and yet, fundamentally, so alike?

Unless we have a view of life that transcends or includes death, there will be fear and dread about our own lives and confusing bereavement in facing the passing of another. It is an unfortunate though quite revealing thing that many persons turn away from religion because of the "untimely" death of a friend or loved one. As one woman said, "I have believed in God all my life, but with the passing of my husband, my faith is shattered. Now I wonder if there is a God." This proves the weakness of trying to understand God through trouble. We need to begin with God, with an awareness of the universal flow of life, and then look at trouble from this transcendent perspective.

Life is whole; the universe is whole. Even though we may experience this wholeness "in part," there is that of us that is changeless and deathless, that is integrally and eternally involved in the universe. Browning obviously had this in mind when he said, "On the earth the broken arc, in the heavens the perfect round."

Some people might feel that it is terribly negative to discuss death; however, a fear of dealing with the subject could well indicate a bondage to it. It could mean that our faith does not include the wholeness of life that transcends death. If death comes, it must be a part of that wholeness, not a deviation from it. Jesus said, "You will know the truth, and the truth will make you free." In the consciousness of the allness of life, there is freedom from the thought of a locked-in existence and from the barriers of birth and death. When, in our thought, we break down the ends, life suddenly becomes a continuing experience of the universal flow. And then death loses its "sting."

Sitting on a pier that extends out into the ocean, one is impressed with the constant flow of the ocean currents, and the formation of waves that start as small swells and move in with increasing size and power. Finally, the waves crash on the shore in a tremendous surge of foaming water. What is a wave? Is it a body of water? Watch a piece of flotsam as the wave passes it by. If the water were actually moving, the flotsam would move with it.

A wave is the ocean expressing as a wave. It has form and shape and movement; it has identity and uniqueness, but it is no more nor less than the ocean. It is not even limited to a particular segment of ocean. It is a movement within the ocean, a projection of the ocean, which at the same time moves on and through the ocean. When the wave crashes on the shore, where is the ocean water that formed the first swell? Right back there in the deeps where it always was, as proved by the flotsam that is still languishing there.

Your life that appears to begin with birth and end with death is like one instant in the movement of the wave. In that instant the wave is a particular part of the water. In this moment, life for you is your body. But life is not limited to your body. If your body should be laid aside in the experience we call death, it is not the end of you or the movement of life that is being projected through you and as you. The wave moves on. Thus it is not possible to understand life unless we are willing to look squarely into and through this thing called death.

Through the marvelous facility of memory, you can look back through your life and remember fragmentary accounts of life's continuous flow. It is as if you had a motion picture film, which was made up of innumerable frames, and then centered your attention on one or two individual frames here and there. Each one is a record of something that happened. There is no point in denying it, nor actually in glorifying it. No one picture tells the story of your life, nor should it be representative of what you are. Each must be seen in the context of the whole, for life is a flow.

Judging life by appearances, you may focus on times of tragedy or failure or unhappiness or injustice, you may understandably conclude that life has been hard. But if you "judge righteous judgment," seeing all things in the context of the whole flow, you will rejoice that life is good. Often the darkness is the prelude to a dawn of light, and the tragic loss opens out into growth and gain as "all things work together for good."

Shakespeare says that the world is like a stage on which we all are actors. During your lifetime you have played many parts and worn many costumes. Unfortunately, you may have identified yourself with one particular role. An actor refers to this as being "typed." An example is the experience of

Boris Karloff, the great dramatic actor, whose career was thwarted because no one could ever afterward see him as anything but the monster of Frankenstein. You may have typed yourself as a failure or an incompetent because of some experience "back there" in your earlier life.

However, there is a flow of life. You are not the same person today that could be seen in isolated frames of past years taken out of context of the motion picture of your life. Take one sequence of thirty years ago where you may appear bumbling and shy. This is not really you at all. It is simply a mark you left in passing. Why let it be a final grade? Yet isn't this precisely what you do if you say, "Oh, I might as well accept my limitations. That is just the way I am." Is it really the way you are? Or is it the frustration of what you are? These experiences were part of a flow. You are not the same person you were as a child or as an adolescent or as a young married. You are already very different in body, mind, and spirit than the person you were a year, a month, or even a few hours ago when you started reading this book.

Can we assume that this process of the flow of life is limited to the brief span between birth and death? Are we to believe that at birth a brand-new product comes forth from some celestial soul factory which plays its little part for a few years and then is swept up in the dustpan of oblivion? Life in this context would make very little sense. And because of the inequities of individual experience, life would be very capricious and unjust. For this reason, religion has always been an outgrowth of humankind's attempt to see beyond death. The very word *Providence*, which has often been used as a name for God, literally means "seeing forward." Somehow, we have always innately felt that life is eternal and that death is not the final thing it appears to be.

Schopenhauer says that the Western world is haunted by the incredible delusion that humankind was created out of nothing and that our present birth is our first entrance into life. He is suggesting the idea of reincarnation. The delusion he refers to has come about due to the misinformation about Christianity. Primitive Christians for three hundred years followed the belief of rebirth through reincarnation. The doctrine was eventually rendered anathema by church fathers for obvious reasons. For if an individual has his own eternal relationship in the flow of life, what of the intermediary of the church and its priesthood?

Victor Hugo wrote:

For half a century I have been writing my thoughts in prose and verse and history and philosophy . . . . But I feel I have not said the thousandth part of what is in me. When I go down to the grave I can say... "I have finished my day's work," but

I cannot say, "I have finished my life." My
day's work will begin again the next morning. The tomb is not a blind alley; it is a
thoroughfare. It closes on the twilight, it
opens on the dawn.[1]

In the flowing experience of life, change is
constant reality. In every change, we see evidence
of the process of death and rebirth. Paul said, "I die
every day!" (1 Cor. 15:31) And of course! Every
day the sun sets to mark the close of one day. We
retire to bed and give ourselves to restful sleep. The
day and all its concerns are over. But day opens
unto night, which in turn opens unto day. At
daybreak there is the return of light, and we plunge
into the hope and promise of the new day.

When a person moves from one room into
another, it could be said of him or her, "He is
leaving a room," or "She is entering a room." Both
are true. We may give it any emphasis we want. In
the same sense, when a student leaves college, she
could say, "My life is over," or "I am beginning a
new life." The emphasis she gives will have a lot to
do with her thoughts and ultimately her whole
experience of life. The same is true through the
changes brought on by marriage or illness or a new
job or even unemployment. There is a death of that
which was, and the birth of that which now is.

It could be said that death is the other side of life,
and life is the other side of death. In the flow of

eternal life, the motion picture continues, perhaps in another reel or scene or chapter. Could it be that a transcendent Self looks out through the eyes of an infant and sees with the unconscious wisdom of a previous life . . . and that the loved one who passes from the sight of our eyes and the clasp of our hands may be on the way to an inexorable new birth?

To some people, this may seem to be a weird notion, and we are not suggesting here an indepth study of this field. Charles Fillmore cautions that the study of reincarnation is not profitable: not what you have been but what you now are is the issue. Yet he believed in it completely. It is a helpful and hopeful thing to know that the flow of life continues beyond the "shadow of death."

In his immortal *The Prophet*, Kahlil Gibran says:

> Should my voice fade in your ears, and
>   my love vanish in your memory ....
> I shall return with the tide,
> And though death may hide me ....
> Forget not that I shall come back ....
> A little while, a moment of rest upon the
>   wind, and another woman shall bear
>   me.[2]

The important thing is to know that you are an eternal expression of the universal flow and that there is no beginning and no end to you. Thus knowing that you are going to live forever, you can let go your apprehensions and anxieties about death and get on with the business of living your life one day at a time.

Jesus said, "You, therefore, must be perfect, as your heavenly Father is perfect" (Mt. 5:48). This is a clear command, giving us the ultimate goal in life. But how can we achieve perfection in one span of seventy-five or even one hundred years especially when we all start at different levels? What of the persons born blind or crippled or brain-damaged? Are they, too, to be held accountable for the degree to which they achieve unfoldment of their perfect Self in one span of life? It is unjust . . . and unthinkable.

It seems obvious that Jesus' command suggests the ultimate toward which we all must work. Yet how many achieve the goal in their lifetimes? How many perfect people do you know? Isn't it more realistic to assume that Jesus was implying that through births and rebirths the goal remains constant and that we are given all eternity in which to achieve it? It is a startling concept and yet a highly credible one, if we can just let go our prejudices. It is a view that opens the way to a sense of the justice of life, the order and continuity of the universe. It is an attitude that takes us out of the littleness of petty themes and selfish affairs.

And it is a view that has been held by vast

numbers of religionists, philosophers, scientists, and poets all through the ages, including: Plato, St. Augustine, Plotinus, Shakespeare, George Bernard Shaw, Goethe, Wagner, Schweitzer, Jung, Spinoza, Robert Frost, Gandhi, Edison, Emerson, just to name a few.

At the heart of this concept of rebirth is the ideal that there is that of you that is more than your body, and the you that transcends the body, the eternal, ever-living soul of you has woven the body temple and is the sustaining influence of it. But if the body becomes unfit for further service and is laid aside in the process that we call death, this is in no way the end of you. The *you* that is more than your body moves on to be "clothed anew according to God's purpose."

The question may persist, "But where do we go from here?" We must remember that what we call "here" is merely the objectified state of that which we are. The "here" is how much of the "within" we have unfolded and the "condition" in which we have brought it forth. We do not really go anywhere from here. And yet in the Father's house are many levels of consciousness. The "where" question pertains to three-dimensional time-space experience. It is the horizontal experience of life. However, beyond the point that we call "death," there is no horizontal movement, for the vehicle for moving is laid aside. Now the flow is vertical, in the formless, timeless, and spaceless realm.

This is why all attempts to explain or describe the experience of death, or even life after death, are meaningless. For descriptions invariably pertain to horizontal experience. Where do we go? The important thing is that we do go on in the flow of life. Man is a multidimensional creature. In the horizontal movement, we are conscious of only three dimensions. We may have existence on many more. In his play *Lazarus Laughed* Eugene O'Neill articulates the problem of one who has returned from the "other side" in describing a fourth or fifth dimension in understandable three-dimensional terms. Lazarus is speechless, so he simply "laughs" at the paradox of man's worry and strain of frustrated living when there is so much more in the flow.

Obviously, all this is not easy to realize when you stand before the casket containing the physical form of one whom you have loved. But if it is disturbing to you, it is because your understanding of life is not broad enough to encompass life that transcends birth and death. You are disturbed because you are out of the consciousness of the flow. Lift up your eyes and embrace a larger sphere. Know the Truth of the limitless flow of life. God is life, in whom there can be no beginning and ending. There can be no death in God, and thus there can be no death, in terms of finality of life, for your loved one.

Sir Edwin Arnold's translation of lines from *The*

Bhagavad-Gita suggests the vision of Eastern religions:

> Never the spirit was born; the spirit shall
> cease to be never;
> Never was time when it was not; End and
> Beginning are dreams!
> Birthless and deathless and changeless
> remaineth the spirit for ever;
> Death hath not touched it at all, dead
> though the house of it seems![3]

One of the most beautiful illustrations of the flow of life is to be seen every day in the rising and setting of the sun. Recall, if you will, a time when you paused at the close of the day to witness a breathtaking sunset, with flaming hues of red spread across the whole sky. It is interesting to reflect on the full context of that which the sunset is only a part. Imagine while you are looking westward, thrilling to the sight of this sunset, a peasant farmer in distant Thailand looks out from his thatched hut to view the hope and promise of a new day in the sunrise. At the same moment you look westward and see a sunset, and he looks eastward and sees a sunrise. And you both stand on the same earth and look at the same sun.

Of course, the sun does not really rise or set at all; it only seems to do so from where you view it. But it is an interesting reflection on life—where experiences actually have no identity of themselves. They become to you what you see them being. No experience ever comes all packaged and labeled as "good" or "bad," "happy" or "tragic." A thing is good or bad because that is the way you see it, and thus that is what it becomes as far as you are concerned.

In the esoteric teachings of antiquity the terms *east* and *west* have an interesting meaning. Looking westward refers to seeing the appearances, dealing with life at the circumference. Looking eastward means looking within, looking to God, dealing with life at its depth. In every experience, the choice is ours—whether to look westward or eastward. Westward viewing leads to anxiety and stress and grief. Eastward viewing leads to faith and understanding and the consciousness of the flow.

When a loved one has passed on, there is an obvious sunset as the light and love of your friend drops beneath the horizon of human communication. As darkness fills the sky, you may be moved with feelings of loneliness and desperation. But the darkness is in your consciousness. There can be no darkness in God or in an expression of God. This loved one has "come to pass," but he or she does not move from light into darkness. It is rather a movement "through the valley of the shadow of death" into the light of a new birth. And death is the "brief drifting of a cloud across the road he or she travels on through which our loved one passes from sunlight into sunlight."Our beloved is in the flow of life.

When you feel the darkness of grief, it is a sign that you are out of the flow, and the darkness is solely within you. Turn about where you are and look to the east, which means to look to God, get into the flow. If you are torn with a terrible sense of loss, it is because you have become overly dependent for love and support from without through this person, and thus you have unconsciously gotten out of the flow. So, now *be still and know . . . you are in the flow.* Loose her and let her go in the movement of her eternal experience toward a new birth. Let go and walk on! In the flow of life, you may go forward to find new love and new opportunities for creative involvement.

Death is not a dead-end street, either for the one who passes or the one who remains behind. Let there be no sad good-byes. How much better to bid our friend, "Good morning—and Godspeed on your way." There is no need to wallow in grief. There are those who hold that grief is a mark of respect, almost like a duty that you should perform. This is nonsense! Of course it is natural to have feelings of sadness, but the sadness should be tempered with the joy of knowing that your loved one is in the flow of life and that he or she goes onward to meet his or her good. Any prolonging of grief, any attempt to hold on to one who has passed, is a mixture of guilt and anger, and it is to be totally out of the flow of life yourself. Turn away from the sunset, face eastward to the sunrise of a new day, and walk on!

There is much interest today in the so-called "spirit world" into which departed ones go and in attempts to make contact with loved ones through psychic means. There is much conjecture relative to the realm of the departed dead and the stages that take place between death and rebirth and between this world and other worlds. Of course, there is much to learn in our quest for Truth. But it may be that we should take one step at a time and one world at a time, that we should work toward self-knowledge and self-discipline in dealing with this frame of experience before we go off chasing shadows in a nebulous "other world."

The question is often asked, "Is it possible to contact the spirit of one who has died?" There is little question of the possibility of spirit communication, though there is much quackery and outright fraud in this field. But there is serious question about the advisability of such practice even through valid mediumship. Departed ones have "come to pass." Life goes not backward but forward. They should be permitted to move on to their next experience. Any kind of holding on in an attempt to make contact with them can serve only to hold them back in their journey. And the psychic dabbling can certainly keep you unnerved and confused, holding you back from your own need to walk on to the next step in your own growth.

This is not to reject the importance of valid research into the process of death and the possibility of new birth through reincarnation. It is an important field for study. If you can be objective in your study, there is much information to be gleaned, though it will mean ferreting through an overwhelming mass of misinformation. But when you are subjectively involved through your own apprehension about death or through a grief-motivated desire to contact a loved one, then there is little that is constructive to be gained and the whole of your stability of life to be lost in such a quest. You might do well to keep out of the graveyard and give your time and attention to the flow of life in the full sunshine of experience on this plane.

What of funeral services? The most important piece of advice is to work out a philosophy that can lead to decisive action. Too often people wait until the crisis comes and then they turn helplessly to a funeral director who then moves the whole experience into a traditional, depressing, and extremely expensive process. Funeral customs in America are the most pagan aspect of our society, based, as they are, on ancient practices of the worship of the dead. But don't blame the undertaker. This industry has flourished by reason of the human tendency to overplay the mourning involvement through confusion and guilt.

Don't ask the funeral director what you should do for your departed one. How can he or she be objective? The worth of the casket or burial plot or floral pieces have absolutely nothing to do with your respect or your obligation. There are some things the state law requires, and there are certain things other members of the family may insist upon. The important rule: Keep it simple and dignified. Cremation is becoming increasingly popular, if that is the word. It may be the best way to dispose of the garment of the flesh that has been laid aside. It can be done (and should be) without flourish or morbidity.

The ideal is to have some kind of "memorial service" where the friends can join in a time of prayer and commitment. It is inadvisable to have the casket present, and certainly it should never be left open if it is present. It is possible to cosmetically make the deceased look "so very real," but why? It only provides another moment of sadness and the urge to hold on. The memorial service can be held at the funeral home, but it need not be. Once the decision is made not to have the casket present, a simple service can be held anywhere.

Here is a good example of a funeral service that was a source of inspiration and light instead of sadness and gloom. The deceased had created a lovely garden in which he had spent many leisure hours nurturing unbelievably beautiful flowers and shrubs. So the service was held right out in his garden—a brief time of prayer and remembering through the fruits of his handiwork. There was no eulogy nor sad preachment, just a few words helping people to understand the meaning of the flow of life that transcends death, and a united prayer-blessing for the loved one in his continued journey. Then the friends went into the house and had a sumptuous buffet and a happy time of fellowship, showing their respect for the departed one, not in sadness, but through the kind of social involvement that he loved.

But don't wait until an experience of bereavement comes to search for answers. Get a well-rounded insight into life that actually includes death. Reflect much on the idea of the flow of life that cannot be locked in between birth and death. Break down the barriers by knowing that on the other side of birth is a flow of life that has "come to pass," and on the other side of death is a flow of life that leads to new birth. Get the sense of being radiantly alive in a continuing and eternal experience in the flow.

Then you can begin to really live one day at a time. You can live each day as if it were the only day of all eternity. Yesterday no longer exists, and tomorrow and the days of the future will simply unfold out of the continuous flow of the experience that is now in its unfoldment.

And in the flow, you can be about the business of growing and unfolding, going through a continuous experience of happenings in this life and a continuous cycle of re-embodiments through all time, moving from frame to frame in the flowing motion picture of your eternal existence.

Notes

1. Living Life From Within-Out

1. John Bartlett, *Bartlett's Familiar Quotations*, Little, Brown & Co., Boston, 15th ed.,1980, p. 69.
2. Ralph Waldo Emerson, "Worship," *The Complete Writings of Ralph Waldo Emerson,* William H. Wise & Co., New York, 1929, pp. 584-585.
3. Eric Butterworth, *Unity of All Life*, Harper & Row, New York, 1969, p. 100.
4. Robert Browning, "Paracelsus," Part I, *The Poems of Browning*, Houghton, Mifflin and Co., Boston, n.d., p. 18.
5. Ella Wheeler Wilcox, "Resolve," *Poems of Passion,* Albert Whitman & Co., Chicago, n.d., p. 128.

2. The Healing Stream

1. Bartlett, p. 298.
2. William Shakespeare, "Julius Caesar," Act I, Sc. 2, *The Complete Plays and Poems of William Shakespeare,* Houghton, Mifflin and Co., 1942, p. 1017.

4. The Effusion of Light

1. Bartlett, p. 397.

2. Robert Frost, "The Road Not Taken," *Complete Poems of Robert Frost,* Holt, Rinehart and Winston, New York, 1961, p. 131.
3. Emerson, p. 167.
4. Arthur M. Abell, *Talks With Great Composers,* G. E. Schroeder, Garmisch-Partenkirchen, 1964, p. 21.
5. Emerson, p. 207.
6. Elizabeth Barrett Browning, "Aurora Leigh," *The Poems of Elizabeth Browning,* Houghton, Mifflin and Co., n.d., Boston, p. 372.

6. The Wellspring of Giving

1. Kahlil Gibran, *The Prophet*, Alfred A. Knopf, New York, 1959, pp. 19-20.

7. Life Comes to Pass

1. William Shakespeare, "Macbeth," Act I, Sc. 3, *The Complete Plays and Poems of William Shakespeare*, p. 1187.

8. To Grow Old or Grow Onward

1. Robert Browning, "Rabbi Ben Ezra," *The Poems of Browning,* p. 383.

9. Life, Death, and Rebirth

1. Victor Hugo, *Reincarnation in World Thought*, Julian Press, New York, 1967, p. 292.
2. Gibran, pp. 83, 94-95.
3. *The Bhagavad-Gita* or *Song Celestial,* in James Dalton Morrison (ed.), *Masterpieces of Religious Verse*, Harper & Brothers Publishers, New York, 1948, p. 603.

About
the
Author

Eric Butterworth celebrates over fifty years as a minister in the nondenominational, nonsectarian movement of Unity. He has had a distinguished career as a communicator in a movement primarily devoted to helping people to discover their innateness and "to alter their lives by changing their thoughts." Discovering early the power of radio, he has been broadcasting on a daily basis for forty-four years. His broadcast, aptly called "Eric Butterworth Speaks," has been beamed via CBS radio to most major cities in the United States. An interesting facet of the universality of the Eric Butterworth message is that he was invited by the Mormon Church to give a daily morning talk on their worldwide shortwave radio network. His voice opened the day's broadcast as a kind of benediction. This continued for many years.

Eric Butterworth has been devoted to finding new and original ways of communicating what he calls "the new insight in Truth." He has long been considered as one of the, if not the, leading creative thinkers and spokespersons in the Unity movement.

Author of fourteen books, most of them still in print; one of them, *Discover the Power Within You* (Harper & Row), is considered as a classic in the field of New Thought. In addition, he has published hundreds of articles and essays. One reviewer says that Eric Butterworth is truly a twentieth century Emerson. He is published in four languages.

He speaks every Sunday in Lincoln Center's vast Avery Fisher Hall. Prior to coming to New York, he served successfully in Detroit, Michigan; Pittsburgh, Pennsylvania; Rockford, Illinois; and Kansas City, Missouri, including service in the U.S. Army.

Eric Butterworth is often asked when he is going to retire. His reply is always the same, "Retirement is for going backwards, and life is only lived forward."

Printed in the U.S.A.

53-0710-75C-1-99